TRUSTING ENOUGH TO
PARENT

TRUSTING ENOUGH TO
PARENT

Replacing Fear with ActiveTrust
as You Raise Your Children

WAYNE HASTINGS

Cook Communications

Faith Parenting is an imprint of
Cook Communications Ministries, Colorado Springs, Colorado 80918
Cook Communications, Paris, Ontario
Kingsway Communications, Eastbourne, England

Cover and Interior Design: iDesignEtc.
Cover Photo: The Stock Market
Editor: Gary Wilde

3 4 5 6 7 8 9 10 Printing/Year 04 03 02 01 00

Library of Congress Cataloging-in-Publication Data

Hastings, Wayne.
    Trusting enough to parent / Wayne Hastings.
    p. cm.
    Includes bibliographical references.
    ISBN 0-78143-410-6
    1. Parenting. 2. Parenting—Religious aspects—Christianity. 3. Trust. 4. Trust in God. I. Title.

HQ755.8 .H377 2000
649'.1—dc21   99-087068

Contents

DEDICATION

This book is dedicated to my children,
Jennifer Rebecca Cook, Zachary Todd Hastings,
and my son-in-law Deron Allen Cook.
You are three special people, given to your mother
and me by God. You are precious in His sight and ours.
I thank God that He allowed me to be your dad.
This book is also for my wife, Pam. You changed my life,
and together we have created a beautiful family.
Thank you for your endless love, trust, support, and prayer.
Without your encouragement this book would still
be in my head instead of on paper.

ACKNOWLEDGMENTS

I have so many people to acknowledge and thank. First, I need to thank my Lord and Savior Jesus Christ for forgiving me and for loving me. Nothing would happen without You and Your steadfast love. Pam, Jennifer, and Zachary, to whom I dedicate this book. Thank you for being my family, for your prayers, support, and for providing all the great stories in this book.

Many thanks to my parents, Ray and Catherine Hastings. You gave me solid teaching and role models to follow.

I have several friends who have made a significant difference in my life:
- Glen and Marilyn Heavilin, for modeling to us when we were young Christians what it meant to be Christian parents.
- My spiritual advisors and friends, Ron Potter, Bruce Johnson, Dan Benson, Steve Potratz, Tim Blair, Margaret Jensen, Leisha Joseph, and Joe Questel. Thank you for always being there for me and for the solid friendships we have.
- My small group, Phil and Suzanne, Del and Ginger, and Ron and Karen. Thank you for your patience with your absentee teacher, and for your encouragement and prayers.
- My teachers and friends, Patsy Clairmont and Florence Littauer. Thank you for all the time you spent teaching and serving others.
- My pastors and friends, Larry Poland, Gary Hardin, and Ron Salsbury. Thank you for being such men of God and for being His man to teach us and lead us.
- Several people at Chariot Victor Publishing need to be mentioned for their support and patience. Many thanks to Randy Scott, Lee Hough, Greg Clouse, and Gary Wilde.

foreword

My friend, enter these pages knowing that this is not a common textbook. It is instead a trusting-book, a tender-book, a turning point-book: one that has the content to influence forever your parenting approach. This isn't a glance-book but a guidebook, for Wayne Hastings has not only been thorough on his topic, but as a parent he has also been through it—through the sometimes twisting labyrinth of parenthood. Which truly heartens me. I appreciate the experienced traveler who has left the safety of the train, has backpacked the trails, has experienced the pitfalls, viewed the vistas, and knows the safest way back to the station.

From the moment I first met Wayne I was impressed with his passionate faith in Christ, his dedication to his family, and his sincere interest in others. He has the enthusiastic heart of a learner, the purposed ear of a student, the wisdom to walk in truth, and the good humor to laugh along the way—all the qualifications of a fine leader. Add to that Wayne's good fortune to marry an exceptional woman, Pam, who exemplifies gentleness, grace, and charity, and you can see why this duo can offer insightful and instructive help to those of us experiencing the (sometimes) painful (almost always) privilege of parenting.

I believed Wayne would one day have to write because his zest for transferring liberating truth to others would demand it of him. I have witnessed the joy that spills over him when he grasps a fresh truth and then fervently conveys it to others. Giving an insight to Wayne is much like adding a new corn kernel to a hot pan—explosive with appealing results.

If you're struggling with a child or if your child is struggling with you (mine have—excuse me, do); if things are going well in your home and you want to insure its continuance; if you're a new parent preparing yourself for a strong child/parent future; or you're smack dab in the middle of a crisis; may I recommend *Trusting Enough to Parent*. I believe if you will respond to the truths in these pages you will be uplifted, better prepared, and, when necessary, changed, that you might enter the rigorous joy of parenting and survive sane and satisfied.

God Bless,
Patsy Clairmont

Introduction

Parents need help. We've always known that parenting was a serious, daunting task, but in our day it has become a matter of life and death. Hardly a day goes by without a new, startling piece of journalism reminding us of childhood dysfunction and parental failure. In a recent editorial, the Toledo Blade said:

> Good parenting is time and energy-consuming, and often mentally and emotionally taxing. But good parenting provides immense personal satisfaction, especially when compared with the devastating fruits of bad parenting.
>
> When we see a child kill just for the sake of finding out what it feels like, it is time for the adult in that child's life to pay the price. And it is time for a new era of parental responsibility. If that means 20 years in prison for the sins of the child, so be it.[1]

Jail time for bad parenting? It may be just around the corner.

Especially in our day, for all the well-known reasons, we must strive for the highest quality of parenting. If you agree, then this book is for you. In fact, this book is for any parent, at every level of expertise, who just wants to do it better.

My wife, Pam, and I have reared two children. It was an interesting (to say the least) time for us and we learned, through trial and error, books, God's Word, and mentors some good and effective approaches to child rearing and family relationships.

I'm convinced that parents—the vast majority of whom are fine people and persons of immense goodwill and impeccable motives—simply need encouragement, practical tools, real-life guidelines, and spiritual support. Too often parents are thrust into a role they know very little about and feel (for some reason) that they should just "naturally" learn. Take it from me, this is simply not true. Parenting takes time, energy, and patience—in fact, it requires all the spiritual fruits almost all at once.

Pam and I have wonderful, loving relationships, and we are so thankful for Zachary and Jennifer. But we learned our parenting skills by trial and error. When we decided to have children, I was scared to death. I'd always thought we would never have children, let alone such wonderful relationships with our children. I look back and can't believe the joy I've had with my kids. However, we weren't prepared or trained—we just brought them home from the hospital and started our crash course in diaper pins and interrupted sleep.

We've made mistakes, and we've seen our share of victories. I'm writing this book (and Pam will have lots of input, as well) to help, encourage, and challenge you. I speak from no ivory tower, nor do I have years of training in child psychology. This book comes from the heart, God's Word, and personal experience. We're in the trenches together.

Overcoming the FEAR

It is my hope that this book contains the kind of practical guidance and biblical references that will help you out of the trap—the trap of fear instead of trust. The recent death of my grandmother helped push me to a point of new understanding of the difference between fear and trust. And I think the distinction is crucial.

Grandmother Nan and I were very close (for many of my growing up years she was a short bike ride away), and her passing was a sad day for all of us. Some time before her death, my mother and father had asked me to preside over Nan's funeral. At the time, I was quite pleased that they asked me, but as the day approached, I must admit some fear and a loss of words (something that rarely happens to me).

One week before Nan's funeral, Pam and I were watching a woman named Joyce Meyer on television. Joyce was talking about fear. She explained that certain fears weren't from God, and that we shouldn't give in to this wrong kind of fear. She defined this kind of fear as Future Events Appearing Real. It will serve as an important acronym as we go into far more detail later in this book. I want to mention this now, though, so you can understand the impact God can make on us when we fully open ourselves up to Him and His teaching.

On the day of the funeral I awoke at 4 a.m. I couldn't sleep any longer; I tossed and turned as thoughts of the coming day kept revolving in my head. I arose at 4:30 and went into my parents' quiet living room. While the rest of the family slept, I opened my Bible and it fell open to Psalm 118. There in the stillness, alone with God, I read:

Give thanks to the Lord, for He is good;
For His lovingkindness is everlasting.
Oh let Israel say, "His lovingkindness is everlasting."
Oh let the house of Aaron say, "His lovingkindness is everlasting."
Oh let those who fear the Lord say, "His lovingkindness is ever-
lasting."
From my distress, I called upon the Lord;
The Lord answered me and set me in a large place.
The Lord is for me; I won't fear;
What can a man do to me?
The Lord is for me among those who help me;
Therefore I shall look with satisfaction on those who hate me.
It is better to take refuge in the Lord than to trust in man.
It is better to take refuge in the Lord than to trust in princes . . .
The Lord is my strength and song,
And He has become my salvation.[2]

As I sat there, all the fear and emotion welled up inside of me. I cried, and I realized that Joyce Meyer had been right. I feared something man-made, not something that should be feared, but something inside my head that might not even happen. All of the people at the funeral were either family or good, long-term friends. Nan was my best pal; what was there to fear?

As I prayed, God revealed some wonderful things to me. I want to capture them in this book as encouragement to parents because I firmly believe that the wrong kind of fear separates us from our children and has a truly negative effect on our precious relationship with them.

Taking Up TRUST

Another event strongly influenced me as I prepared to write this book. I was asked to give a devotional talk at my company's board meeting. I decided to speak about how Jesus related to people in His ministry, how He extended encouragement, training, hope, and love. We're all business people with staffs, and I wanted the Advisory Board to get a glimpse of Jesus as the ultimate servant leader—surely He could point us toward certain basic principles of "human resource management."

God, as He often does, had other plans.

The night before I was to give my talk, I awakened with a start. It was 2 o'clock in the morning before a busy day of important meetings, but there I was, wide-awake in my hotel room. Now, I must say that I'm a very light sleeper, and usually when I travel, I don't get a full night's rest. This night, however, was very different. I felt something strange surrounding me and I was encouraged, by the Holy Spirit, to get up and out of bed.

Once I was out of bed, I couldn't stop thinking about Psalm 118 and that morning before my grandmother's funeral. Repeatedly in my head the Scripture tumbled and tumbled. What was fear? Why was I fearful about anything? I sat and prayed, thanking God for His care for me.

As I prayed, another thought came to mind. The opposite of fear is . . . trust. As I looked for verses in my Bible about trust, another acronym came to me. Trust is Truly Relying Upon Scriptural Truth. I couldn't believe it; I usually don't think in terms of acronyms; however, God had given me a real gift with this one! Only He could have awakened me and only He, at this moment, could have revealed this new truth to me. I was awestruck and I praised God.

As I sat in my room, I was further encouraged to completely change my devotional talk. I didn't need to communicate about employee relations; instead, I needed to communicate God's definition of fear and trust. Therefore, with the time now approaching 3 a.m., I completely rewrote my message.

Next morning, when I spoke, I couldn't believe the board's response nor my level of energy. The spirit in the room was wonderful, and many of the members had tears in their eyes. It was

God's message and the perfect time to deliver that message. These were business people confronted with obstacles everyday. Did they fear? Absolutely. Did they need to be reminded of God's form of trust and fear? Absolutely.

We will look at trust later in chapter 2 of this book. However, I can say that parents who are motivated by FEAR (as I defined it above) instead of TRUST miss out completely on God's best for them and their children.

A third event, just a few days later, would move me not only to see God's hand in my life and the writing of this book; it would also challenge me to jump into battle—a battle for parenting.

Entering the Fray

April 20th, 1999, found me in an airplane heading for a meeting in Colorado Springs. When I got into my hotel room after the flight, I turned on the television and the local news was broadcasting a horrific story. Thirteen people had died and 23 had been injured at Columbine High School. The Colorado media was never-ending in its coverage of the event. Professional sports stopped in Denver; people everywhere in the hotel were talking about the tragedy. I read this later on a website:

> *On April 20, 1999, Eric Harris and Dylan Klebold walked into Columbine High School and shattered our hearts. Before they took their own lives, they had taken the lives of 12 students and one teacher, left 23 wounded, and written a question mark on the face of the world: "Why?"*[3]

Another website said:

> *Today is April 20, 1999. The news on the radio and television is focused almost entirely upon the tragedy at Columbine High School in Littleton, Colorado. The questions on everyone's minds seem to be:*
> *1. Why did this happen?*
> *2. Where did the tools these perpetrators used come from?*
> *3. Why didn't anyone see what they were up to?*

4. How can we prevent this from happening again?[4]

These were the questions and comments from Colorado citizens. When I went to my meeting, Columbine was an important subject, and many people at the office I was visiting knew someone at Columbine or living in Littleton. People wanted to express their grief, and they desperately wanted answers.

I have read somewhere that human beings are separated from each other by six levels or degrees. In other words, everyone knows everyone within this six-layer triangle. In my experience, Christians are about two or three degrees or levels away from each other, and nowhere was this more apparent than in Colorado on the day after the Columbine tragedy.

At dinner that evening, a colleague and I continued our discussion of the prior day's events. Both of us are parents, and our conversation seemed to center around the Columbine parents. Where were the parents of the boys who inflicted all this pain? We had heard radio newscasters talking about the boys and how separated they apparently were from the mainstream of the school. Broadcasts showed their homes and nice neighborhoods. Yet nothing much came forward about the parents' roles in these two young men's lives.

As my colleague and I continued to talk, I shared my recent illumination about TRUST and FEAR. The more I shared, the more I realized that God had some new purposes for this lesson. This was not another devotional or middle of the night message from the Holy Spirit. This was something more, and it could and would affect parents.

Trusting Enough to Parent

It strikes me that we as parents are overly fearful. Fearful of our children, fearful of making grave mistakes, fearful of the right kind of discipline, fearful of getting involved, fearful of reaching out and trusting God to rear these wonderful gifts bestowed upon us. In many cases, we don't reach out to God, take His Word firmly in our hands, and trust Him to do the right things in our families. That is the basic premise of this book.

It is my deep-felt desire to challenge you to forget about FEAR and move toward TRUST in your parenting. Fear paralyzes. It can cause us to miss the most special human relationship (outside of marriage) that we will ever have. Fear isn't of God, and fear will keep us from being the parents only He could create.

The chapters that follow are meant to help you move from FEAR to TRUST. Yes, I know that moving forward is always a scary thing. It will likely involve significant change. But take God's hand . . . and let's go together!

Wayne A. Hastings
November, 1999

Notes

1 "Punish the Parents," *Toledo Blade*, February, 1999.

2 *The Open Bible* (Nashville: Thomas Nelson Publishers), New American Standard Edition.

3 From HYPERLINK http://users2.ipa.net/~1turley/library/schtragedy.html.

4 From HYPERLINK http://www.billpalmer.com/colorado.htm.

Chapter 1

VACATIONING AT CAPE FEAR?

I LOVE OLD MOVIES. I guess it's something my mother taught me. She grew up in the golden age of Hollywood, and as a child, going to the movies was a great family outing for her and her family. We always had fun times together watching movies. She introduced me to Fred Astaire, Laurel and Hardy, Clark Gable, Cary Grant, and a host of other stars from that era. For me, there's still nothing like watching an old movie. Sure, some of the new ones are OK, but it's hard to get excited about them when you compare them to *Casablanca* or *Gone with the Wind*.

One favorite of mine is *Cape Fear*. The original starred Robert Mitchum and Gregory Peck. I know a remake was released a few years ago, but the original film noir classic shows fear at its best. A creepy ex-con (played by Robert Mitchum) has developed a seething hatred for the attorney who put him in jail (Gregory Peck). After Mitchum threatens to harm Peck's family, there begins what one movie reviewer called "a fascinating game of crisscrossing ethics and morality."[1]

Robert Mitchum is not only a creepy ex-con; he *is* fear. He uses tricky mental games to get inside Gregory Peck's head. He can make a glance or a subtle body movement communicate terror and relentless torment. Peck, on the other hand, is a model citizen, having done nothing wrong. He works hard, loves his family, and has established himself as an upstanding citizen in a small southern town.

Peck is not unlike many of us. He's trying hard to live his life in a good way. He's putting out great effort to be a moral, upright, community-minded citizen. He's not out to hurt anybody. He is a picture of us, today, in our homes or workplaces.

Mitchum on the other hand? He's laughing. He sneers at Peck and does so many things to subtly change Peck's thinking and his ability to logically get out of the problem.

Isn't that just like fear?

WHAT IS FEAR?

Yes, fear seems to laugh at us, taunt us, and force us to move out of our strengths and right into our weaknesses. It causes us to lose our confidence. It sneers and keeps coming at us until we break its hold upon us or succumb to paralysis.

Why do I begin this book by talking about fear? Because the frightening kind of fear is our enemy, and we need to thoroughly understand it in order to improve our parenting skills. Let's face it: when it comes to parenting, we have many fears. *Will I do it right? Will I make a big mistake that will "damage" my child for life? Will I have terrible regrets once the kids are out on their own?* I have had such thoughts, and I'm sure you could add your own to the list. Yet, if I speak of fear, I must also, right from the beginning, speak of God's power in our lives to overcome our terror. It is a power that gives us guidance, wisdom, and clear-thinking whenever we need it. It is an awesome force that has defeated fear and can continue to overcome it daily in our homes. With God's power, we will be good parents.

How thankful we can be that when fear strikes and we recognize it, we can back off and let God handle it. We (unlike Peck) can be renewed and strengthened as a result of our battles with fear. But we've got to be willing to face fear head on. So let's take some time to examine three kinds of fear that come through to us in the Scriptures.

Frightful Fear

No doubt about it, feeling scared and frightened is the work of the devil. My dictionary defines this kind of fear as "a feeling of alarm or disquiet caused by the expectation of danger, pain, disaster, or the like; terror; dread; apprehension." It is an emotion that runs through us and propels us into all sorts of negative behaviors.

Danger, calamity, alarm, and pain all get our adrenaline flowing because God gave us a special warning system that kicks into gear whenever we encounter something that causes us to be afraid. What's worse is that some of the things we fear actually come true. Many times, however, what we imagine is far worse than what ever could happen in reality. Fear gets a grip on us, a firm grip, and we become its victim while fretting over events or circumstances that never materialize.

Depending on our experiences in life, one person's fear could be another's thrill. Don't believe me? Visit a theme park that has wild scary rides. My wife and I just visited one, and we had differing opinions on what was fun and what constituted real fear. On one ride in particular, the park takes your picture just before your car plunges into the water. In that photo, one of us is laughing and the other is shrieking in fear. Fear for one of us can be excitement for the other.

As a little boy, I really wanted to be a cowboy. I had the guns, hats, and chaps. I was ready to take to the trail. However, one day a photographer with a pony came to our neighborhood. My mom got me all dressed up in my finest Roy Rogers' cowboy get-up. Guess what? When I finally got up on that horse, I couldn't stop crying. I was scared to death of it and wanted no part of the picture or the pony. Here I was, all ready to take on Dodge City . . . until I sat on that pony. Chuck Swindoll writes:

A college friend of mine . . . worked several summers ago on a construction crew, building a hospital in Texas. He was assigned to the twelfth story and was given the job of helping a welder who was welding the flooring structure made of huge, steel beams. So scared of falling, my friend literally shook with fear every day, though he admitted it to no one. One hot afternoon the welder looked up and noticed the man shaking in his boots. He yelled, 'Are you scared, son?' The student stuttered, '—-s-s-s-scared! I've been t-t-t-trying to tell you for t-t-two weeks that I q-q-quit.' [He was] frozen with fear.[2]

The King James Bible mentions the word fear over 380 times, and often it means the kind of fright I experienced on that horse so long ago—it's the idea of being terrified. In the original Greek it is the word *ekphobos* and literally means "frightened outright." The writer of Hebrews uses the word in Hebrews 12:21, in the context of Moses giving the Law on Mount Sinai. The people to whom he was writing were Hebrews who had turned to Christ. (It must be remembered that the early church—the three thousand who were saved on the Day of Pentecost—were not Gentiles but Jews. Until Paul and Barnabas and the other early missionaries began to move out, the early church for those first few years was nearly 100 percent converted Jews.)

Now these converted Jews in Jerusalem who had turned to Christ found themselves at a great loss. They had been accustomed to going to the temple. They had been accustomed to hearing the Mosaic Law read to them. Now they were shut away from the Law, and now they were shut out from the temple. They were no longer a part of the old system at all, and they must have felt very much on the outside. Therefore, I think the writer is saying to them: "You come now to a mount that is different from Mount Sinai, and you do not want to go back to that." Mount Sinai was the place where the Law was given and three thousand people were slain (see Ex. 32), but three thousand people were saved on the Day of Pentecost. There was death at the giving of the Law; there was new life when the Gospel was preached on the Day of Pentecost. The giving of the Law was by no means a delightful experience. There were thunder and lightning, earthquake and storm, blazing fire and the blast of a trumpet that grew louder and louder and louder. It was a terrifying experience—so much so that the people said to Moses, "Speak thou with us, and we will hear: but let not God speak with us, lest we die" (Ex. 20:19).

So, the writer of the Hebrews uses *ekphobos* to describe Moses at Mount Sinai: "The sight was so terrifying that Moses said, 'I am trembling with fear'" (Heb. 12:21). He was in awe of God, certainly, but he was also very much afraid at the same time. It was a scary place, and nobody would be foolish enough not to be afraid, or in fear during such an event.

I talk about this only to give you some insight into fear. Yes, it is OK to be afraid. Moses was afraid, yet God gave him the Law. King David was afraid when Saul sought his murder, but David was also known as "a man after God's own heart." Being legitimately afraid is not primarily what concerns us in this book.

Awesome Fear

Our English word "fear" is the translation of several Old Testament words. With that in mind, consider the most used form, the word that expresses reverential respect. In Genesis 20, Abraham is faced with a real problem. He is sojourning in Gerar with Sarah, but is afraid of Abimelech the king of Gerar. Therefore he conveniently tells Sarah to lie for her sake (really his sake) and tell the king an out-and-out lie. Well, the king finds out about the ruse, and guess what excuse Abraham uses? He replies to Abimelech's scolding, "I said to myself, 'There is surely no fear of God in this place, and they will kill me because of my wife'" (Gen. 20:11).

What is Abraham talking about? He is using the Hebrew word *yirah*. It means "reverence" or "awe." Most often, *yirah* is used to describe "the fear of God." Such fear is certainly a prominent element in Old Testament religion, even synonymous with religion itself. Psalm 34:11 says, "Come, my children, and listen to me, and I will teach you to fear the Lord" (NLT). In Ecclesiastes 12:13 Solomon writes: "Here is my final conclusion: Fear God and obey his commands, for this is the duty of every person" (NLT). Clearly, God expects and demands our attention to this detail.

So there it is. Awe and reverence of God lead us to wisdom— and who couldn't use a little wisdom when it comes to parenting? We are told not to start anything until we have gained sufficient "fear" of the Lord.

The two types of fear we've discussed, being terrified and being in awe, are not of themselves bad or good, nor do they get in the way of effective parenting. However, when we look at the next type of fear, we will see some possibilities for damaging results in the parent-child relationship.

Flighty Fear

In the New Testament, the fundamental word for fear in the Greek is *phobos*. It's where we get our word "phobia" and can mean "fear," "terror," "affright." *Phobos,* however, can also mean "flight," that which is caused by being scared, or "that which may cause flight." Our typical parenting fears are not awe, not sheer terror, but a deep feeling of wanting to avoid, or run away from, the problem or concern. The meaning indicates a choice—either we can stay and face the concern, or we can run from it.

I think of the Apostle Paul in this regard. He probably wanted to run away many times. Look, for example, at 1 Corinthians 2:1-5 (TLB):

1 Dear brothers, even when I first came to you I didn't use lofty words and brilliant ideas to tell you God's message.
2 For I decided that I would speak only of Jesus Christ and his death on the cross.
3 I came to you in weakness—timid and trembling.
4 And my preaching was very plain, not with a lot of oratory and human wisdom, but the Holy Spirit's power was in my words, proving to those who heard them that the message was from God.
5 I did this because I wanted your faith to stand firmly upon God, not on man's great ideas.

Can you relate to being "timid and trembling"? What do you do then? One Sunday our former pastor decided to let his associate pastor preach. The associate was so very nervous that he was literally pacing in his office when I happened upon the scene. I saw our senior pastor put his arm around the associate and say, "Look here, my friend, for that hour and for those services, you are God's man! Stand firm on what you are saying. You prayed about it, God responded, now deliver it."

What a wonderful antidote to the fear factor! The young pastor just wanted to run away. Instead, his elder was cheering him on, encouraging him to present what God had laid on his heart.

Paul must have felt the same way as he wrote the Corinthians in this letter. He was fearful *(phobos)* and he felt like running away. But he did not run away. Instead, he delivered a powerful message to these Christians of Corinth. Deep within his own weaknesses, Paul knew he alone was not sufficient to preach to these believers. His success was from another power source, from divine power.

Paul, like our associate pastor, had prayed and prepared. Now it was his time to deliver the message, and he did it. Not by his own strength, but through the power of God, he chose to stay and preach. He chose to stay and change lives. He chose to stay and confront those new believers.

FEAR NOT!

As a worship leader some years ago, I was attracted to a song. It had such a driving tempo and meaningful lyrics that I could easily bring it to mind when I felt like fleeing a fearful situation. The song is "Fear Not."

> *"Fear not, for I am with you; Fear not, for I am with you;*
> *Fear not, for I am with you," says the Lord. (repeat)*
> *"I have redeemed you, I have called you by name, Child,*
> *you are Mine. When you walk through the waters, I will be*
> *there,*
> *And through the flame you'll not (No Way!) be drowned.*
> *You'll not (No Way!) be burned, for I am with you."*[3]

Isn't that a wonderful promise? A God who is faithful, who calls me His child. A God who challenges me to "fear not!" Whenever we see "fear not" in the Bible, we can be sure the text is not talking about *yirah,* the reverence or awe of the Lord. God is never telling us to not respect Him and have awe in our hearts when we spend time with Him. He wants us, in everything we do, to "fear" Him that way. But He will not let *phobos* destroy us if we depend on Him.

We can take a lesson from Jehoshaphat when it comes to learning how to confront that kind of fear. In 2 Chronicles, Jehoshaphat is giving instructions to some newly appointed judges. He says:

> *5 He appointed judges in the land, in each of the fortified*
> *cities of Judah.*
> *6 He told them, "Consider carefully what you do, because*
> *you are not judging for man but for the LORD, who is with*
> *you whenever you give a verdict.*
> *7 Now let the fear of the LORD be upon you. Judge care-*
> *fully, for with the LORD our God there is no injustice or*

partiality or bribery."
8 In Jerusalem also, Jehoshaphat appointed some of the
Levites, priests and heads of Israelite families to administer
the law of the LORD and to settle disputes. And they lived
in Jerusalem.
9 He gave them these orders: "You must serve faithfully
and wholeheartedly in the fear of the LORD.
—2 Chronicles 19:5-9 (NIV)

Jehoshaphat decided to set everything up around God. What is interesting to me is that the judges of this court were some of the Levites and priests who were most learned in the law. They were celebrated for their wisdom and held great integrity among the people. These were also some of the chief fathers of Israel. Matthew Henry regards them as "peers of the realm,"[4] which means they were persons of age and experience who had been men of business. These men would serve to be the most competent judges of matters of fact, as the priests and Levites were of the sense of the law.

But look at Jehoshaphat's admonition. He tells them to fear the Lord. He tells them to respect and revere God. Not to flee. His charge, in verse 9, is simple: they must see to it that they act from a good principle and they must do all in the fear of the Lord. They are admonished to always set Him before them, and then (and only then) would they act faithfully, conscientiously, and with a perfectly upright heart.

There was another admonition. According to Matthew Henry, "They must act with resolution. 'Deal courageously, and fear not the face of man; be bold and daring in the discharge of your duty, and, whoever is against you, God will protect you: The Lord shall be with the good.' Wherever he finds a good man, a good magistrate, here will be found a good God."[5]

No, it is obvious that God does not want us ever to lose sight of our awe and respect for Him. We could find many other texts demonstrating His desire for us to revere or respect Him. *What He wants us to do is stop running away.* "Fear not, for I am with You" is not only a great song lyric, it is a command with a promise. It is saying, "Don't flee from what's bothering you, FOR I AM WITH YOU!"

So, what are our fears about our children? God says, fear not and know that I am with you. Before going on, let's look at one more "fear not" chapter in the Bible. We'll simply move ahead with our story of Jehoshaphat as he faces some interesting problems.

The Battle Is the Lord's

In 2 Chronicles 20, we see a glorious account of God recognizing a person who is totally dependent upon Him. God delivers Jehoshaphat in such an exciting way that it leaves no doubt in anyone's mind that divine intervention was at work. However, Jehoshaphat has a crisis, and in that crisis he learns an invaluable lesson. In the beginning of chapter 20, the Moabites, Ammonites, and some of the Meunites[6] came to make war against the people of Israel led by our hero, Jehoshaphat. Jehoshaphat declared a fast and sought God's help. He acknowledged God's sovereignty over circumstances and went into the best mode for problem solving—fasting and prayer.

Verses 6 through 12 are a prayer offered by Jehoshaphat to the Lord, reminding Him of His promise and asking for His presence. I'm sure it was hard to understand why God, the sovereign King over all nations, would allow these pagans to come up against His covenant people, who were led by a God-fearing king. God's hasty intervention seems to be expected in such circumstances.

Isn't that just like us? Don't we question why God allows certain circumstances or problems to come along? We are God-fearing people, so why do we have to go through this? We go to church, say and do the right things, so why must we wade through this ocean of daily problems? Many of us ask these questions all the time, and I am certain the people then were asking similar questions. Basically, they were afraid. But verse 13 reminds us that "all the men of Judah, with their wives and children and little ones, stood there before the Lord" (NIV).

They were afraid, but they stood there before the Lord. They chose not to run but to stand in front of a loving, sovereign God and pray. Then the prophet Jahaziel speaks:

15 He said: "Listen, King Jehoshaphat and all who live in Judah and Jerusalem! This is what the LORD says to you:

*'Do not be afraid or discouraged because of this vast army.
For the battle is not yours, but God's.
16 Tomorrow march down against them. They will be
climbing up by the Pass of Ziz, and you will find them at
the end of the gorge in the Desert of Jeruel.
17 You will not have to fight this battle. Take up your posi-
tions; stand firm and see the deliverance the LORD will
give you, O Judah and Jerusalem. Do not be afraid; do not
be discouraged. Go out to face them tomorrow, and the
LORD will be with you.'"*
—2 Chronicles 20:15-17 (NIV)

This Levite, Jahaziel, whose origin can be traced back to David,
delivers a message of encouragement and unbelievable hope. He
speaks directly to the king, looks him straight in the eye, and says,
"Fear not! The battle is God's." He inspired the people to go out
against this enemy (or speaking to us today: another crisis in parenting), trust God, and He would make them more than conquerors.
What a guy! Where was this prophet when I had to teach my kids
to drive? Or, worse than that, let them drive off solo for the first
time? (Actually, he was right in the Word, waiting for me.)

Jehoshaphat that day conquered an army of enemies. He put his
faith in the Lord, and God gave him a great victory. The combination of prayer (20:3-13), prophecy (20:14-17), and praise (20:18-22)
brought him wonderful success.[7]

God delivered Jehoshaphat because of this man's unique ability
to listen and let God have the battle. We can take a profound lesson from this king. We can learn to "fear not," give the battle to
God, and trust Him to give us victory. As our children have grown,
we have faced many battles. Some small, some large, but battles
nonetheless. It is very easy to allow circumstances to control our
responses instead of listening to Jahaziel's advice and allowing God
to fight the battle.

In the middle of conflict, my strength is the Lord. Jehoshaphat
felt no fear because he realized that the battle was the Lord's.
Author and pastor Tony Evans writes, "When Satan attacks, you
don't have to fight him all by yourself. Just be faithful to do what
God has asked you to do, and there is Somebody on the other side

of the heavenlies to take care of the enemy for you."[8] That is what it means to let the battle be God's—to simply proceed down the road with all of our human ability and insight, while recognizing that the destination is totally in God's hands. In fact, we *expect* that the outcome will be just right and that we'll be used to the fullest in bringing it about. We calmly accept, as we take each step, that we won't necessarily be able to see over the next hill or around the next corner. We are proceeding by faith, after all.

As I told you in the introduction to this book, my grandmother's funeral brought quite a bit of fear into my life. A couple of weeks before the funeral, I was watching Joyce Meyer's television show, and she was teaching about fear. She pointed out that fear is, for all practical purposes, Future Events Appearing Real. She explained that we feel like fleeing from a circumstance or a problem when we allow our imaginations to take control of us and project future disaster as if it were actually set in stone.

Then we have to deal with all the anxious feelings that arise. In the grip of fear, we are shaky, our mouths are dry, we get heart palpitations. This happens because we see a future full of dreadful things. We see a disaster around every corner. And what makes it worse is that we see these things and believe we cannot handle them.

When our kids were young, we lived on an extremely busy street. It was a major east-west thoroughfare and also a city bus route. I can remember Pam and I spending so much time lecturing the kids about that street. Why? Because we could envision them riding their bikes or running after a ball or chasing a neighbor across that street . . . and surely they'd be hit by a car. Fear is future events appearing real.

How about when the telephone rings in the middle of the night? Whether or not the kids are out of the house or snuggled down in their beds sawing logs, when that phone rings in the middle of the night, my heart starts pumping, the adrenaline starts flowing, and I'm on the edge. Why? Because I envision something terrible has happened. Somebody is calling to deliver bad news and "where are the kids?" Fear is future events appearing real.

We are going to spend lots of time in this book talking about how to combat fear. For a moment, let's look at the piece of

Scripture that helped me so much to conquer the fear before my grandmother's funeral.

Therefore, I Will Not Be Afraid

As I shared earlier, I was so fearful the day of my grandmother's funeral. I awoke at four in the morning and was haunted by self-doubt and anxiety. I was paralyzed by the fear that I would verbally stumble at the podium. I was scared that I wouldn't communicate the right message, that some people who needed to hear a clear Gospel message would walk away without it. I so wanted to honor the woman who had invested so much time and energy into my life, and I was panicky thinking that I'd drop the ball. I was simply looking ahead and imagining the worst.

Therefore, in my distress, I read Psalm 118, a beautiful piece of poetry that overflows with thanksgiving. It was sung by worshipers as they proceeded into the holy temple and therefore embodies lofty elements of praise as it calls upon the past and stresses God's deliverance. Some commentators believe this is the last song Christ sang before His death.

Verses 5 through 14 were a great encouragement to me on that lonely morning. I was alone in my parents' living room. I just opened my Bible and it flopped to this psalm. I read:

5 In my anguish I cried to the LORD, and he answered by setting me free.
6 The LORD is with me; I will not be afraid. What can man do to me?
7 The LORD is with me; he is my helper. I will look in triumph on my enemies.
8 It is better to take refuge in the LORD than to trust in man.
9 It is better to take refuge in the LORD than to trust in princes.
10 All the nations surrounded me, but in the name of the LORD I cut them off.
11 They surrounded me on every side, but in the name of the LORD I cut them off.
12 They swarmed around me like bees, but they died out

as quickly as burning thorns; in the name of the LORD I cut them off.
13 I was pushed back and about to fall, but the LORD helped me.
14 The LORD is my strength and my song; he has become my salvation.
—Psalm 118:5-14 (NIV)

According to verse 5, the psalmist is in real trouble. He is in a place of distress, literally a tight place. So how does he handle his fear? The psalmist chooses not to allow future events to appear real. He chooses God instead of letting random, fearful thoughts invade his thinking even though all sides seemed to be pressing upon him.

Similarly, I felt as if I were surrounded by people who might be critical or hurtful. I felt as though I would surely buckle under the pressure and fail. So what did this psalm say I can do at such times?

• *I can call upon the Lord—always, at any time.* First, David says, "I cried to the Lord." That seems so simple, but how often do we forget to turn to God? There was a powerful tool available to the psalmist, and he used it. He called upon the Lord. Remember Jehoshaphat? What did he order first? He called upon the Lord. Prayers of distress leap out of our hearts and directly into the heart of God. I remember my prayer that early morning. I was in torment, in anguish, and I just buried my head and called upon the Lord.

As with David, the Lord answered me and set me in a large place. *The Message* reads, "Pushed to the wall, I called to God; from the wide open spaces, he answered." God is never shut up. The Hebrew word here is *merchab,* and it connotes wide expanses. God brought me out of a very narrow point of view, a personal confinement to fear, and put me in a place of liberty and freedom, His broad expanse.

• *I can constantly remember: The Lord is on my side.* Literally translated, verse 6 reads, "He is for me." Sitting alone in my parents' living room, it struck me that for a short time, I was God's appointed man. If I just realized that He was on my side, I would be successful.

Because the Lord is on my side, I need not fear. This doesn't mean that difficult times become easy or that there will be no suffering. Yet we still need not fear. We can be calm and confident, though surrounded by enemies, because the Lord is on our side. What can circumstances, people, and events do to me? Nothing, if I let God be at my side. For then, even physical death—as scary as it is—comes with the promise of resurrection.

• *I can sing powerfully—when the song is His.* When I speak of singing here, I'm talking about acting with courage in any situation where God is my strength. David said: "The LORD is my strength and my song."

At the funeral, I decided to sing two songs. My grandmother left me a legacy of music, and I thought it was only fitting to sing for her at the grave side. It was without a doubt the most difficult time of my life. Fortunately, my son agreed to play guitar along with me. I will never forget his steadfastness and help. But even with Zach by my side, I was scared. I wanted to run away. I had projected a future event—*I may be off key, I may stumble, I may hit a bad note on my guitar.* My mind whirled out of control until I realized it was not "my song."

It was not my strength that mattered. Victory belonged to a different source that day. Just as Jehoshaphat's victory was the result of God's presence, so were my simple songs. He carried me through it. As with the psalmist, God was my salvation; the songs were His.

Unknown to me there was a professional, flamenco-style guitarist at the funeral. After the service he came up to me and said, "Great job; I don't think I could have done that." I thanked him and realized that I had not done it either. The Lord had helped me overcome my fear—it was His song.

As parents, I know there are times when we have so little strength. We face monumental circumstances and fears. Each of us worries about our children and hopes that we can do our very best in a job for which we have had no training. Some of us have, at times, had so little strength that we were ready to faint (or run away). We don't feel like singing—to ourselves or to an audience. However, when God's strength is revealed and salvation comes, then our song will be clear and in perfect tune. It will be full-voiced and glorious.

THINK AND TALK ABOUT IT

1. What fears about parenting are you facing today?
2. Recall and discuss a time when Future Events Appeared Real. Did those events materialize?
3. What practical steps could you take this week to trust the Lord with your fears each day?

Notes

1 Review excerpted from: http://www.amazon.com.

2 Charles R. Swindoll, *Living Beyond the Daily Grind* (Nashville: Word Publishing), 96.

3 Phil Pringle, *Fear Not*, © 1984 by Seam of Gold. Admin. by Maranatha! Music.

4 *Matthew Henry's Commentary on the Whole Bible* (Peabody, MA: Hendrickson Publishers, 1991), 745.

5 Ibid., 745.

6 According to the *New Commentary on the Whole Bible*, "These people were an Arab tribe whose home normally was on the edge of the Arabian desert. They may have come from Ma'an, about twenty-two miles southeast of Petra on the ancient caravan route that led from Damascus to Mecca. This hostile people at one time had oppressed Israel (Judg. 10:12), and they were later attacked by both Hezekiah (1 Chron. 4:41) and Uzziah (2 Chron. 26:7)" Quick Verse 5.1.

7 Warren Wiersbe, *Expository Outlines on the Old Testament* (Colorado Springs: Chariot Victor Publishing), in QuickBooks 5.1

8 Tony Evans, *The Battle Is the Lord's* (Chicago: Moody Press, 1998), 96

Chapter 2

WHO DO YOU TRUST?

I CAN'T BELIEVE WHAT MY PARENTS USED TO DO. My father wore a business suit every day to work, so we had a lot of dry cleaning, and the local cleaners offered a delivery service. All my mother had to do was call and they'd send somebody by to pick up the dirty clothes and drop off the clean ones. Well, Mom so trusted the company that she simply left the back door open for them. It didn't matter if we were home or away running an errand; the delivery man came right into the house for the clothes through the unlocked back door.

I can't imagine anyone being so trusting today. I know I'd never give an unknown delivery person free access to my house—though probably no company these days would allow an employee to enter a home unsupervised. How many times have you had to stay home from work because a repairperson was coming? We just don't trust that person, and the company doesn't, either.

Who *do* you trust anymore?

A sign in an English country inn sums up how much we trust today. It reads: "Please introduce yourself to your fellow guests since we are one big happy family. Do not leave valuables in your room."[1] That little wall plaque perfectly illustrates the paradox under which we operate today. We want to feel like one big happy family, but in reality we're all guarding our valuables. We want to reach out to our neighbor, but we don't trust what the neighbor might ask of us. We want to be loved, but we don't trust the other person to love in return.

And wouldn't you agree that trust is a big issue in our families today, certainly a crucial quality for effective parenting? In order to be the most effective parents, we must learn to trust. For one thing, we need to rely on God as our refuge and strength, the One in whom we can place our complete confidence and hope. When we are blessed with children, we're naturally fearful in the face of our awesome task of leading those children into adulthood. It is only through TRUST (Truly Relying Upon Scriptural Truth) that we can accomplish what God has called us to do.

WHAT IS TRUST?

We spent some time in the previous chapter looking at the various aspects of fear; now we'll focus on trust—trust in the Almighty God to make us good parents. If you were to ask me to define "trust," I'd immediately want to explain four of its primary qualities. . . .

Faith: Undergirding Daily Trust

For our discussions, I want to draw a distinction between faith and trust right at the beginning. In some instances, they may be the same, but for the purpose of this chapter's analysis, let's set the two concepts apart.

Faith comes *before* trust. I'm going to assume that without faith, a person cannot trust. Faith is forever, while trust is daily. Faith is an umbrella, while trust is one of the spokes of the umbrella. For our purposes in this chapter, faith is once and for sure, while trust is something that may need to be addressed every day, every hour, or (in severe crisis) every minute or second.

The Book of Hebrews says, "This faith is the firm foundation under everything that makes life worth living. It is our handle on what we cannot see. The act of faith is what distinguished our ancestors, set them above the crowd."[2] Faith is the anchor to our relationship to God; trust is the outworking of that faith.

The great life question for us becomes: How fully will we learn to trust God before entering heaven? As we will see, trust is fleeting, and we can choose, with every decision that comes our way, whether to trust or worry, trust or fear. We can even trust in one area of our life and then, when some other difficulty crops up, choose not to trust.

Yes, trust can be fickle; faith is forever.

Confidence: Trust through Action

The Hebrew word *batach* is one of two words used in the Old Testament to express trust. Some scholars believe that the word is rooted in ancient Arabic, giving it this meaning: "to be stretched out, taut." The basic idea, then, is firmness or solidity. *Batach*, according to the *Theological Wordbook of the Old Testament,* "expresses that sense of well-being and security which results from having something or someone in whom to place confidence."[3] This word is never associated with "believe" but rather with "hope." In the positive sense, it means "relying on God." In the negative, it can mean relying on something or someone deceptive. The word, therefore, does not infer faith, but stresses a safe or secure feeling or an "unconcerned" feeling.

The Old Testament is full of stories demonstrating confidence in God as opposed to the folly of placing confidence elsewhere. Psalm 31 points out that trusting in the wrong thing will lead to disgrace and shame. In this psalm David shows his confidence in God and seeks His help, reaching out and asking the Lord to be his rock. He pleads to be pulled out of the net and commits his spirit to God. He knows God and realizes that God knows and stands by His people in adversity as well as in prosperity. In verse 8, David avows that God did not abandon him to his enemies. In verse 9, David breaks into a prayer: "Have mercy upon me, O LORD, for I am in trouble: mine eye is consumed with grief, yea, my soul and my belly." Was David, indeed, "in trouble"? Consider:

- He stayed with Saul, and Saul tried to kill him twenty-one times;
- He stayed with his enemies for a brief time;
- He fought in many wars;
- He was a backslider;
- He had tremendous family troubles;
- He had a rebellious son;
- He had many other calamities and difficulties.

In other words, David had seen more than his share of troubles! At this point, "David was beaten all the way down, until there was no way to look but up."[4] He was feeling so low that he felt it in his belly and soul—a reference to his extreme feelings of grief within his circumstances.

However, David decides to trust (batach) God. He had trusted other things; now he was ready to trust the Lord. When he looked up, there was God. David put his full confidence in his maker. "God is at work here. He is rerouting David's life . . . what a turning point!"[5] David asks God to be his confidence, and experiences renewed strength and security.

Generally speaking, people who put such "trust" or confidence in God receive many benefits: They are delivered from their enemies (Ps. 22:4); they receive answered prayer (1 Chron. 5:20); they walk straight paths (Prov. 3:5); they live with a feeling of joy and gladness (Ps. 16:9); they know inner peace and an absence of fear (Ps. 4:8).

We put our confidence in God, not other things or other people. God is the leader, the figure of absolute trust, and God delivers tremendous blessing. The reason? Not because of our merit or anything we have done, but because of God's everlasting loyalty to His people. God has an infinite kindness and graciousness that permits Him to extend blessing when we trust.

Years ago I taught a finance class in Sunday School. When we got to the section about tithing, the class members made a commitment to tithe and in so doing, to absolutely trust God with their families' finances. We couldn't believe the miracles that came as a result of that commitment. It seemed that every week one couple or another would tell about personal victories, not only with their finances, but also in other areas of their lives because of trusting God and tithing. All of this in the midst of an economic downturn that was seriously affecting our entire community. A few couples in the class were either unemployed or forced to work part-time.

One week, a couple came into class just beaming. They'd really suffered because of the economic downturn and were struggling to make ends meet. They'd decided to tithe and trust God for the rest. When Sue (not her real name) went into the grocery store that week, her checkbook balance was pitifully low. She prayed, because they needed food and she was beside herself. As she prayed, God gave her confidence as she put her trust in Him. She went down each aisle and made wise choices. She kept her mind focused on God's promised provision, and when she went to the cash register was so surprised to have a basket full of groceries. When she went to pay, she was shocked to discover that this shopping basket full of food had cost her less than $25. She had $30 left in her account.

Refuge: Trusting the Sheltering Arms

The Hebrew word here is *hasa*. It occurs fifty-six times, predominantly in the Psalms. Its root means "to take refuge in" and denotes a sudden action. It may be derived from the common experience of fugitives, or men at war, when they seek safety among the hills or strong rocks, a place to which they can run for cover when the battle intensifies. *Hasa* has been used to describe the act of taking shelter from a storm or fleeing from danger to the high country.

How does this look in our lives today? Chuck Swindoll writes:

> *You just discovered your son is a practicing homosexual. Where do you go? Your mate is talking separation or divorce. Your daughter has run away for the fourth time . . . and this time you are afraid she's pregnant. How about when you've lost your job and it's your fault. Or, financially, you have blown it. Where do you go when your parent is an alcoholic? Or you find out your wife is having an affair? Where do you turn when you flunk your entrance exam or you mess up the interview? Who do you turn to when you're tossed in jail because you broke the law?[6]*

We look at these questions and realize that right now, right here in the midst of our own hot battles, we need a refuge. And God is, above all, a refuge. He is the rock, the shield, and the wings that give us protection. Here are some Scripture reminders:

- He is our refuge (Ps. 14:6).
- He is our shelter (Ps. 61:3).
- He is a fortress (Ps. 91:2).

Psalm 118 gives us an interesting contrast:

*8 It is better to trust in the LORD than to put confidence in
man.
9 It is better to trust in the LORD than to put confidence in
princes.*
   —Psalm 118:8-9

It is better to trust *(hasa)* in God than it is to put confidence
(batah) in man or princes. It is better to allow God to be our shelter, our absolute stronghold than to put confidence in things that are
not God. If we take refuge, God will also take our part and our side
in the struggle.

Remember Psalm 31 and David? Under the heading of confidence, we pictured the restoration of David as he put his confidence
in the Lord. Let's look at Psalm 31 again and consider what else this
marvelous psalm can tell us.

*1 Lord, I trust in you alone. Don't let my enemies defeat
me. Rescue me because you are the God who always does
what is right.
2 Answer quickly when I cry to you; bend low and hear my
whispered plea. Be for me a great Rock of safety from my
foes.*
   —Psalm 31:1-2 (TLB)

David says, "Lord I trust *(hasa)* in You alone. You alone are my
refuge; let me settle beneath Your shelter, and please don't let my
enemies defeat me." In God, and under the shelter of His protection, David found peace and security. He was able to move from
refuge to confidence because he knew at that moment that God
would defeat his enemies—whatever they might be. To seek refuge
stresses the insecurity and self-helplessness of even the strongest of
people. David sought shelter where others would find a trap if they
didn't fully understand that God's refuge was a blessing and easily
available to them.

Why not share David's shelter in the One he called My Strength,
Mighty Rock, Fortress, Stronghold, and High Tower. David's refuge
never failed. Not even once. Moreover, he never regretted the times
he dropped his heavy load and ran for cover. Neither will you.[7]

Hope: Trusting the Unseen Reality

In the New Testament, we see trust explained in one additional way. It comes through in the Greek word *elpis* and it is often translated "hope." *Elpis* most often means "a favorable and confident expectation." It has to do with the unseen and the future. Such "hope" describes: the happy anticipation of good; the ground on which "hope" is based; the object upon which "hope" is fixed.[8]

During our lives, we hope for many things. As children, we hope that others will like us. At Christmas we hope for a special present. As teenagers, we hope we won't get acne, or, in some cases, we hope nobody notices. As young adults, we may hope to get into a good college, and once we do, we hope we make it through the strenuous curriculum. Then we hope to find a mate, hope to have children, hope they are born healthy. The cycle continues.

Biblical hope is somewhat different. It can be described as a trustful expectation. It is the anticipation of a favorable outcome under the protective wings of God. More specifically, hope comes from seeing what God has done in the past and applying that to future events. It is not a guarantee of a positive outcome, but rather a positive assurance that God has worked in the past and will continue to work in the future. Here's how writer Frederick Buechner describes it:

> *Hope stands up to its knees in the past and keeps its eyes on the future. There has never been a time past when God wasn't with us as the strength beyond our strength, the wisdom beyond our wisdom, as whatever it is in our hearts— whether we believe in God or not—that keeps us human enough at least to get by despite everything in our lives that tends to wither the heart and make it less than human. To remember the past is to see that we are here today by grace, that we have survived as a gift.*[9]

This contrasts greatly with the world's definition of hope, doesn't it? The world sees hope as a *feeling*. It is a positive attitude, based upon no historical grounds, that things will just work out. The world's definition of hope is all wrapped up in "me." I want something to happen; therefore, it will, because I want it that way. On the contrary, the biblical definition of hope is based upon the firm foundation of God's character and His plans. In this light, hope is either an optimism with no foundation, or trustful expectation grounded in God's saving acts.

Biblical hope has three characteristics that I'd like you to keep firmly planted in your mind as you approach your parenting task:

•*First, hope is the result of experience.* In the Book of Romans, Paul writes:

1 Therefore being justified by faith, we have peace with God through our Lord Jesus Christ:
2 By whom also we have access by faith into this grace wherein we stand, and rejoice in hope of the glory of God.
3 And not only so, but we glory in tribulations also: knowing that tribulation worketh patience;
4 And patience, experience; and experience, hope:
—Romans 5:1-4

Paul is saying that we are put right with God and have peace through our daily relationship with Christ. Then, in verse 2, we are not merely introduced to God by Jesus Christ for an interview, but we are to remain with Him as part of His household. Then Paul brings us to a stark reality. He reminds us that tribulations bring us patience, and patience leads to experience. The word "experience" (*dokime* in the Greek) indicates the effect of proving, or probation. So hope, then, comes from a process. It is the result of our experience.

This is an important point as we look at trusting and its effect on the fear in our lives. Trust involves action; I don't know how anyone can gain experience without actually *doing* something. If we fear something or someone, we must gain some experience in handling that situation. Only then will we have the historical base to move forward and trust in new areas of our lives.

•*Second, hope triumphs over difficulties.* Let's look at Romans once again:

15 for the Law brings about wrath, but where there is no law, neither is there violation.

16 For this reason it is by faith, that it might be in accordance with grace, in order that the promise may be certain to all the descendants, not only to those who are of the Law, but also to those who are of the faith of Abraham, who is the father of us all,

17 (as it is written, "A FATHER OF MANY NATIONS HAVE I MADE YOU") in the sight of Him whom he believed, even God, who gives life to the dead and calls into being that which does not exist.

18 In hope against hope he believed, in order that he might become a father of many nations, according to that which had been spoken, "SO SHALL YOUR DESCENDANTS BE."
—Romans 4:15-18 (NASB)

You probably know the story of Abraham and Sarah. Here Paul is using Abraham to explain Gospel faith. Abraham was ninety-nine years old when the Lord appeared to him and told him that He would establish a covenant with him (named Abram at the time) and multiply him exceedingly. In Genesis 17:4 God tells Abram, "You shall be the father of a multitude of nations" (NASB). How surprised Abram must have been! He was quite old, had devised some interesting schemes in order to have children, and now God was telling him that he would be the father of a multitude.

In Genesis 21, Isaac is born. Abram and his wife had gone through a divinely appointed name change and now experienced the birth of their son. Verse 1 of chapter 21 says, "Then the Lord took note of Sarah as He had said, and the Lord did for Sarah as He had promised" (NASB). They appropriately named him Isaac, meaning "laughter."

Now, in Romans 4, Paul points to Abraham to describe the "hope" of the Gospel. It is a great lesson for us, for we can now understand what it means to "hope against hope" as we look to God to help us triumph over difficulties. Abraham heard from God, and his whole being was full of absolute confidence that what God had promised would come to pass. Chuck Swindoll calls it consistency:

Consistency [is] a living model of patience, determination, and strength—regardless of shifty, rootless times. . . . It knows little of ups or downs, highs or lows, blue Mondays or holiday hangovers. It hates tardiness and absenteeism. It thrives on sacrifice and unselfishness. It's an obvious mark of maturity. It's hanging in there day in and day out in spite of everything that could get you sidetracked.[10]

That is a description of hope and how it triumphs over difficulties. You hang in there and have great hope that God will deliver on what He has promised. Having trouble understanding your children? Ask God for wisdom and believe; have hope that He will deliver on what He has said. Don't feel that you are on the right track with your kids? Pray and ask God, then stand back and watch Him work. Whatever it is you need, God will deliver, based upon His word and promises. He certainly did for a 100-year-old man named Abraham.

• **Third, hope's foundation has a solid cornerstone: love.** Loving Christ is an important step to having hope in Christ. A sign of our faith is the love we have for Christ, for how can we truly have hope in His Word and promises if we don't welcome Him and love Him? This type of love is manifested in obedience. John writes:

21 The one who obeys me is the one who loves me; and because he loves me, my Father will love him; and I will too, and I will reveal myself to him.
—John 14:21 (TLB)

Charles Wesley said, "All my requests are lost in one, 'Father, thy will be done!'"[11] It is impossible to have hope without love, and obedience is love in action. Without love of God and Christ, we cannot have the hope necessary to trust completely in God and His Word. First Corinthians gives us the guidelines of love and it finishes in verse 13 with a great triangle relationship:

13 There are three things that remain—faith, hope, and love—and the greatest of these is love.
—1 Corinthians 13:13 (TLB)

So love is the third leg of the stool, the footing to hope and faith. Without it, we don't have the foundation necessary for either. My friend Margaret Jensen, in her book *First We Have Coffee,* provides a wonderful story about her mother and love. Her mom tells it this way:

> *One day Susie came in from the playground, holding a broken pot with a wilted plant in her muddy hands.*
> *She begged me, "Please don't throw away the plant."*
> *"But Susie, the plant is dead," I said.*
> *"Then you must love it back to life, Mother."*
> *She thrust the wilted plant into my hand and skipped away, completely confident that its life would return. I placed the remains of this plant in a new flowerpot filled with fresh dirt. The sun filtered through the Brooklyn skies and warmed the lifeless plant that sat on my windowsill. Every day I watered my little wilted garden and waited. One day a green shoot appeared, and now a lovely green plant thrives on my sill.*
> *When someone brings us a frightened, wilted, hurt child, I hear Susie say, "Love it back to life, Mother!" So many human relationships can be loved back to life.*[12]

Love brings us back to life, love never fails, and love conquers all. Love is the cornerstone of hope; hope is how we trust God.

HOW CAN I PRACTICE DAILY T.R.U.S.T.?

Early in the introduction, I told a story about fear and trust. Remember how it just came to me? Early that morning before our Advisory Board meeting I realized that trust, as opposed to fear, meant Truly Relying Upon Scriptural Truth. The point of my personal study in Psalm 118 was that to overcome our fear, we must hold onto, or completely rely upon, the truth of the Scriptures. Our confidence, our refuge, and our hope all develop more thoroughly as we rely daily upon the truth of God as presented in His inspired Word. It seems so simple, yet it is not an easy thing to do.

The first time our children drove solo was a frightening experience for us parents, an event that called us into heavy reliance upon

God and His Word. If you haven't had this pleasure, let me give you a few points of reference. First, your child is a teenager and many states allow driving alone at age sixteen. That's a scary thought in itself, but add to that the fact that the car will be traveling through traffic, is quite heavy, and can do untold damage to things and people—in effect, it's a lethal weapon! Such thoughts (aided by our fertile imaginations) quickly become overwhelming. Enter God's Word and scriptural truth:

• The children are not mine, but Yours.
• The children were Your gift to us.
• You said You wouldn't give me more than I could handle.
• You said, to trust in You and I would have peace.

I'm sure you could add other promises to the short list above. Certainly, His Word covers teenagers driving cars—and all our fears about that. The hard part is to rely, moment by moment, on His truth to meet every concern, overcome every fear.

Trust in the Lord, Not Yourself

Let's look at a few other fearsome attitudes and how Truly Relying Upon Scriptural Truth can help us conquer them in practical ways. Examine a portion of Proverbs 3 with me:

> *5 Trust in the LORD with all your heart and lean not on your own understanding;*
> *6 in all your ways acknowledge him, and he will make your paths straight.*
> *7 Don't be wise in your own eyes; fear the LORD and shun evil.*
> *8 This will bring health to your body and nourishment to your bones.*
> —Proverbs 3:5-8 (NIV)

We have spent considerable pages describing trust in the Lord. It is the first rule if we are to rely on scriptural truth. Here we have *batach*, and it again means "have confidence in" God. It is no bad plan that this proverb begins with confidence in God.

The word used for "lean" here is the Hebrew *shaan*. It means "to lean on something or someone for support." Ezekiel 29 talks about the inhabitants of Egypt, who only had staffs made of breakable reeds—in comparison to the house of Israel, who had God. The reed is the same word used here for "lean" in Proverbs. Who would be foolish enough to lean upon a breakable reed for support?

The Book of Esther also provides insight into trusting the Lord more than ourselves. Through some unusual circumstances, beautiful young Esther is made queen of Persia by marrying Xerxes. She was a Jewish orphan girl, raised by her cousin Mordecai, and she was queen mother while her stepson Artaxerxes ruled. Under this king, Nehemiah rebuilt Jerusalem. Esther's marriage to Xerxes gave the Jews prestige and made it possible for Nehemiah to leave Persia and build the temple in later years.

There was, however, some scheming going on by a man named Haman. He was a wicked court officer whose day of triumph was short. Haman hated the Jews and succeeded in having the king sign a royal decree that every Jewish man, woman, and child should be killed and all their property taken. Mordecai showed Esther the decree, realizing she was the only hope for preventing the Jews' massacre.

Esther faced a tough decision. She could lean on herself or trust God.

Mordecai asks Esther to appeal to the king to spare the Jews. At the peril of her life, Esther decides to see the king and reveal her nationality in a desperate attempt to deter her husband Xerxes. After prayer and fasting, Esther at last appears before the king. And, as the story ends, Haman is humiliated and Mordecai becomes a national hero—he is elevated and set over the house of Haman. Through Esther's trust and reliance on the scriptural principles of fasting and prayer, the Jews are saved and "massacre day" becomes a day of celebration.

Esther's trusting attitude was reflected in verse 16 of chapter 4: "Go, gather together all the Jews that are present in Shushan, and fast ye for me, and neither eat nor drink three days, night or day: I also and my maidens will fast likewise; and so will I go in unto the king, which is not according to the law: and if I perish, I perish." Like any human being, she was concerned about herself, of course;

nevertheless, she leaned heavily upon God's Word. She trusted Him.

Acknowledge Him; He Will Direct

Proverbs 3 moves on to another method of truly relying upon scriptural truth. It is the concept of acknowledging God and allowing Him to direct our paths. The King James Version mentions "making our paths straight." Ever take a walk down a winding path? If we acknowledge God, He will make those winding paths straight for us.

The Hebrew word for "acknowledge" is *yada*, and it means "to know by thinking; to know by experiencing."[13] Unlike knowing through reflection, this is a knowing through contact. It is knowing through the senses and is experiential. Therefore, hear what the writer of Proverbs is saying: that *first we need to really know God.*

After we know Him, then He promises to direct our paths. We know Him, we trust Him, and then He promises to direct our paths (make them straight). It is the logical progression of a deep relationship with a loving Father. We get to know Him through His Word, observe how He touches our lives, how He answers our prayers, and then we begin trusting Him to guide us through the paths ahead.

Let's look at the experience of Daniel in this regard. In the personal history of Daniel (chs. 1–6), we find three different times of difficulty. First was the testing of the four Hebrews when they arrived at Babylon (ch. 1). Then we see the trial of the fiery furnace (ch. 3). And finally comes the most famous crisis, Daniel landing in the lions' den (ch. 6). In each of these experiences, Daniel and his friends won the victory, but the very first victory lays the foundation for all the others. Since these Jewish boys were faithful to God while they were yet teenagers, God was faithful to them in the years that followed.

The boys had been used to the familiar surroundings of their homeland, and now they are whisked away to a foreign land. Nabopolassar, the father of Nebuchadnezzar and the king of Babylon, died while Nebuchadnezzar was besieging Jerusalem. He had to return quickly to Babylon, leaving his generals to conduct the Jewish captives to Babylon, among whom were Daniel and his companions. So . . . these verses show us the daring test. . . .

8 But Daniel resolved not to defile himself with the royal food and wine, and he asked the chief official for permission not to defile himself this way.

9 Now God had caused the official to show favor and sympathy to Daniel,

10 but the official told Daniel, "I am afraid of my lord the king, who has assigned your food and drink. Why should he see you looking worse than the other young men your age? The king would then have my head because of you."

11 Daniel then said to the guard whom the chief official had appointed over Daniel, Hananiah, Mishael and Azariah,

12 "Please test your servants for ten days: Give us nothing but vegetables to eat and water to drink.

13 Then compare our appearance with that of the young men who eat the royal food, and treat your servants in accordance with what you see."

14 So he agreed to this and tested them for ten days.

15 At the end of the ten days they looked healthier and better nourished than any of the young men who ate the royal food.

16 So the guard took away their choice food and the wine they were to drink and gave them vegetables instead.

—Daniel 1:8-16 (NIV)

Warren Wiersbe explains:

The Babylonians could change Daniel's home, textbooks, menu, and name, but they couldn't change his heart. He and his friends purposed in their hearts that they would obey God's Word; they refused to become conformed to the world. Of course, they could have made excuses and gone along with the crowd. They might have said, "Everybody's doing it!" or "We had better obey the king!" or "We'll obey on the outside but keep our faith privately." However, they did not compromise. They dared to believe God's Word and trust God for victory. They'd surrendered their bodies and minds to the Lord, as Romans 12:1-2 instructs, and *they were willing to let God do the rest.*[14]

We know that at the end of this test, the four lads displayed nice, rosy cheeks and a healthy, robust demeanor. They appeared more handsome than all the others, those who were eating the king's junk food. They stood strong in the face of temptation. Obviously, Daniel and his three friends had never read 1 Corinthians 10:13, but they knew its truth by experience.

Do remember that word "experience." Daniel and his friends had experienced (acknowledged) God, and He had promised to direct their paths. The essential verse comes in Daniel 1:17. One translation reads, "God gave them everything they needed." He made their paths straight. Of course, Daniel had also refused to acknowledge any gods from the Babylonian Empire. He chose instead to acknowledge the God of Israel and to wait for Him to make his paths straight, even in the midst of some terrible moments.

Fear Him; Shun Evil

Verses 7 and 8 in Proverbs 3 call us to a lifestyle. We are to fear (stand in awe of) the Lord and shun evil. We are also not to trust in our own judgment, but fear the Lord as well. What will this do for us? We will have "health to our navel, and marrow to our bones." If I may give the biblical meaning: This is a deep healing and health coming from our umbilical cord (signifying "deep inside" us) to our self—bones—our entire being. Just as the umbilical cord (referred to here as the "navel") gives the child life and nourishment in the womb, so fearing God and departing from evil gives life to a child of God.

This Scripture tells us: stand in awe, don't trust yourself, shun evil, and I will give you deep healing. If we truly trust God, we will obey Him. We may think that our own wisdom is sufficient, but it is not; we need the wisdom of God. Of course, verse 5 isn't teaching that Christians should avoid thinking and considering facts when making decisions, because God expects us to use our brains. Rather, it means that we should not trust our own ideas or wisdom as the final step; we go on from there to ask God to direct us (James 1:5).

This passage in Proverbs puts a cap on Truly Relying Upon Scriptural Truth. We cannot ultimately trust our ways and ourselves.

These verses call us to put ourselves aside and trust God, rely on His Word, and experience His success in all our endeavors with our children.

THINK AND TALK ABOUT IT

1. What do you consider the greatest example of faith you have ever seen? Why?
2. What can help a person overcome fear?
3. How does trust change a person's focus and perspective?
4. In what one area of your life, in which you have not been trusting the Lord, will you begin to trust Him this week?

Notes

1 James S. Hewitt, *Illustrations Unlimited* (Wheaton, IL: Tyndale House Publishers, Inc., 1988), 368.

2 Quoted from Eugene Petersen, *The Message*, Hebrews 11:1-2.

3 *Theological Wordbook of the Old Testament*, Bible Explorer, Version 2.

4 Charles R. Swindoll, *David, a Man of Passion and Destiny* (Dallas: Word Publishing, Inc., 1997), 75.

5 Ibid, 75.

6 Charles R. Swindoll, *Growing Strong in the Seasons of Life* (Portland, OR: Multnomah Press, 1983), 254-55.

7 Ibid., 255-56.

8 *Vine's Complete Expository Dictionary of the Old and New Testament* (Nashville: Thomas Nelson Publishers, 1985), 311.

9 Frederick Buechner, *Christian Reader*, Vol. 35, no. 2.

10 Charles R. Swindoll, *Growing Strong*, 19-20.

11 Edythe Draper, *Draper's Book of Quotations for the Christian World* (Wheaton, IL: Tyndale House Publishers, Inc., 1992), #8088.

12 Margaret Jensen, *First We Have Coffee* (Eugene OR: Harvest House Publishers, 1995), 123-124.

13 *Vine's Complete Expository Dictionary of Old and New Testament Words*, (Nashville:Thomas Nelson Publishers, 1985), 130.

14 Warren Wiersbe, *Expository Outlines on the Old Testament* (Colorado Springs: Chariot Victor Publishing), in QuickBooks 5.1

Chapter 3

TRUSTING ENOUGH TO ENABLE

"PARENT" IS AN ACTION PHRASE, not merely a title given to us when we arrive home from the maternity ward of the local hospital. When you think about it, the idea of parenting someone is a pretty fearful concept. Acknowledging a mere title poses no problem. "Hi, I'm Zach's parent" is easy to say.

But not easy to be or do.

As I've said before, none of us is trained to be a parent; it is baptism by fire, accompanied by loud crying at midnight, countless ear infections, ugly scrapes and bruises, and the occasional broken curfew (be thankful if you avoid broken bones). As someone once said, "If it was going to be easy to raise kids, it never would have started with something called labor."[1] A title can be a passive thing, but a verb connotes action, and we need to be ready for the action—because there will be plenty of it. As newspaper columnist William Raspberry wrote,

> We spend a lot of time on the subject of sex education in the schools. Maybe it's time to introduce mandatory courses in parenting—for boys as well as girls. Parenting skills, difficult enough for the lucky half of us [who were brought up in values-oriented two-parent families] to acquire, are all but impossible for the unlucky half to come by. And yet nearly all of them will become parents. We'd better start doing what we can to help them do it right.[2]

Action—how we act with our children—is critical to enabling

them. I've discovered that parenting has a number of *action-roles*. Practicing them has helped Pam and me to enable our children to become effective and successful adults. To enable means to make possible. In the case of children, we can make possible particular events and outcomes, but we can also make possible a nurturing childhood or "growing up" experience.

As our daughter Jennifer was growing up, she wanted to be an actress. She loved being on stage and tried out for every church and school play. She even spent an entire summer in a little theater group. During that time of her life, we spent a lot of time enabling her to realize her dream. We cleared our calendars of other events and made it possible for her to attend rehearsals, take lessons, and be ready for performances. It took a lot of time and energy for us to interrupt our lives to make all of this possible. However, it was worth the sacrifice, because our involvement and desire to enable focused Jennifer's energy into something she not only *wanted to do* but was obviously *gifted to be*. It was a personal strength of hers to perform in front of people, and we enabled her to stay within her area of strength.

I believe there are at least three action-roles of an enabling parent: serving, teaching, and encouraging. Fulfilling these roles is essential for any parent who wants to make things possible for their children. I realize that not all children are performers or into sports, but every child (and every parent, for that matter) has strengths. The action-roles of enabling help us learn to focus our time and energy to the benefit of our children by magnifying their strengths and diminishing their weaknesses.

ACTION-ROLE #1: SERVING

Matthew 23:11 starts us off in the right direction: "The greatest among you will be your servant" (NIV). The word used for "servant" is the Greek *diakonos*, which means "deacon" or "minister." It can be translated "to pursue serving." It refers to one who carries out the command of another. In the New Testament, it is used of kings, civil governments, men and women of the church, ministers, disciples, and Jesus. But in Matthew 20:27, the writer uses another term for servant. It is *doulos*. This word, as compared to *diakonos*, views servanthood in terms of *relationship to the master*. On the other hand, *diakonos* views servanthood in terms of *relationship to the work.*

The term *doulos* can also mean, "one who gives himself up for another's will."[3] This is the definition I'd like to suggest for the enabling parent. It pictures a parent whose personal agenda takes a back seat (for a time) so the child can be enabled in her area of strength. (Notice I didn't say in the parent's area of strength.) I believe the parent must be willing to put the child's needs before his or her own. Thus parenting becomes an act of "serving" (*doulos*) the child.

I love sports. I've played them all my life and enjoyed every minute of it. At the time our daughter was born, I was playing golf almost weekly. I also belonged to a league softball team that played at least weekly, if not twice a week. I was busy doing my own thing and, using Paul's words, fighting the change that had come into my life. I sure didn't want to give up my sports!

Pam and I talked about it—rather loudly a few times!—until I began to realize that I just wasn't serving my family. Therefore, I decided to put softball and golf on the shelf. Now, in retrospect, I wouldn't trade the family time I created by this decision for any string of holes-in-one or home runs. I can vividly remember some very special times with both Jennifer and Zachary that I probably would have lost if I'd been self-absorbed in those hobbies that regularly kept me away from home.

Saturday, around our house, became Dad's Day. Almost every Saturday, I took over from Pam and was with the kids. From the days he began walking, Zachary would join me in mowing the lawn. He walked right beside me, holding onto the mower, and those memories will be with me for a long time. I learned to be a servant to my kids' needs, being there for them and enjoying every moment.

Let's look at another parent and how she tried her hardest to enable her children . . . but failed. Her story comes from Matthew 20:20-28 (NIV):

20 Then the mother of Zebedee's sons came to Jesus with her sons and, kneeling down, asked a favor of him.
21 "What is it you want?" he asked. She said, "Grant that

one of these two sons of mine may sit at your right and the
other at your left in your kingdom."
22 "You don't know what you are asking," Jesus said to
them. "Can you drink the cup I am going to drink?" "We
can," they answered.
23 Jesus said to them, "You will indeed drink from my cup,
but to sit at my right or left is not for me to grant. These
places belong to those for whom they have been prepared
by my Father."
24 When the ten heard about this, they were indignant
with the two brothers.
25 Jesus called them together and said, "You know that the
rulers of the Gentiles lord it over them, and their high offi-
cials exercise authority over them.
26 Not so with you. Instead, whoever wants to become
great among you must be your servant,
27 and whoever wants to be first must be your slave—
28 just as the Son of Man didn't come to be served, but to
serve, and to give his life as a ransom for many."

James and John's mother, Salome, was undoubtedly responding to what her sons had related as Jesus' own words to them. In the preceding chapter of Matthew (19:28), Jesus promised His disciples that they'd someday sit on twelve thrones, judging the twelve tribes. Salome, probably hearing of this, and understanding it literally, came to request the top leadership roles in this new government for her sons. It appears, in light of Mark 10:35, that she made this request at their instigation.

That is a natural reaction for a parent, don't you think? We hear our children wanting something, and it sounds as if they'll just "die" if they don't get it. So we rush forward with all our might to move mountains and claim whatever they want, right? I would suggest that this type of enabling is off base and wrong.

Salome made a few mistakes, and I think we can learn from them. First, notice what Jesus says in verse 22: "You do not know what you are asking." Salome didn't take the time to understand the situation. She also didn't understand her children's needs, let alone their actual desires.

At one point in his high school career, Zachary wanted to be on the swim team. His school had a tremendous program that asked the students to sacrifice most of their summer and, during school, most of their early mornings. Pam and I approached Zachary's request with a knowledge that Zachary was not a morning person, and he had set some high academic standards for himself as well. Instead of simply agreeing with him, we spent some time learning about the program, contemplating the sacrifice necessary, and examining his deepest personal goals. We then sat down with Zachary and listened to his reasons for wanting to be on the team.

As we listened, we realized that our son wasn't ready for the level of sacrifice and discipline required to compete on that swim team. He loved the water and liked swimming, but it was a quantum leap from enjoying the water to competing with this team. Nevertheless, we let him explain to us how he was going to work it all out. We then presented what we had been thinking: Zachary was certainly old enough to make this decision, we wanted to enable him to make the decision, and we were ready to support him in whatever direction he chose.

It was important for us to gather facts (Zachary's temperament demands facts, not anecdotes) and enable him. After a few days, Zach admitted that he didn't want to give up his early mornings or any of the things he was already involved with at school. Salome, on the other hand, didn't completely take the time to understand what Jesus was saying, and she simply jumped at her sons' initial request without researching the details.

Salome also caused disunity in the ranks of the apostles. Verse 24 of Matthew 20 says the apostles were indignant with John and James. Salome's headlong plunge into her sons' lives (a non-enabling and disruptive approach) not only caused them personal damage, but collateral damage as well. (Isn't this what destroys many churches today? Good intentions lead to whispers and murmurings, then a break in unity caused by unbounded stirrings of animosity.)

Lastly, I must wonder if Jesus wasn't speaking to Salome when He talked to the disciples in verse 25. He speaks of dominion and authority in reference to the Gentiles. These words mean "to lord it over" and "to exercise authority or wield power." I can't help but speculate that Jesus was also directing Salome to enable her children as opposed to lording it over them and others. After all, He alone was their Lord. She had been pushing her sons too strongly in areas that neither she nor her sons completely understood or needed.

A biblical example of the positive results of enabling comes to us through the life of Timothy. As I read the biblical accounts of his spiritual development, it's obvious to me that his great mentor, the Apostle Paul, deeply loved this young man—whom he called him "son"—and that Timothy loved Paul. Timothy had eventually achieved a position of church leadership based upon the spiritual training of his mother and Paul. Timothy's mother must have provided an excellent home environment for Timothy to become the kind of pastor he was, ministering in a rough neighborhood to a crowd of people who were older than he was. He was truly a remarkable young man. However, his growth started at home with an enabler, a teacher, for a mother.

ACTION-ROLE # 2: TEACHING

I'm sure Timothy's mother, Eunice, took every opportunity to teach her son. The Scriptures tell us about a parental "handing down" process that served Timothy well:

> *Your honest faith—and what a faith it is, handed down from your grandmother Lois to your mother Eunice, and now to you!*
> —2 Timothy 1:5 (TM)

Eunice surely taught this young man about Jesus, explained his gifts to him, and no doubt conveyed crucial precepts about responsibility and leadership. Truly enabling parents not only take the time necessary to serve, but they also make certain they are teaching their children along the way.

There is an old story about a mother who walks in on her six-year-old son and finds him sobbing.

"What's the matter?" she asks.

"I've just figured out how to tie my shoes."

"Well, honey, that's wonderful." Being a wise mother, she recognizes his victory in the developmental struggle of autonomy versus dependence. "You're growing up, but why are you crying?"

"Because now I'll have to do it every day," he says, "for the rest of my life!"[4]

This humorous story shows the result of teaching. Parents who are enablers teach their children positive values, daily lessons, life-changing experiences, and practical wisdom that lasts them the rest of their lives. Like teaching a little boy to tie his shoes, wouldn't it be wonderful if we could instill biblical truth and values into our children so they could use them "every day for the rest of their lives? The truth is we can, if we take advantage of every opportunity to enable our children. Those times must include not only communication of biblical truths, but also the communication of life in Christ. Jennifer and Zachary are both adults, yet they still come to Pam and me for advice and wisdom from our experience. They expect us to be ready to answer their questions, and they have come to expect that we relish the opportunity to do so. John Dewey said, "Education is a social process. Education is growth. Education is not preparation for life; education is life itself."[5] Do you agree?

It would be worthless for us simply to push facts and doctrines at our children unless we're also willing to convey life-changing experience along with the facts. The idea is application; without application the truth is great stuff but untied to a powerful vision for positive change.

Years ago I took some graduate school courses, and the class I enjoyed most was a cost accounting workshop. I know what you're thinking: "How boring!" Well, you would probably be right (unless your profession is cost accounting), except for the marvelous professor who made it all so fascinating. This teacher made the subject come alive for all of us by constantly attaching real-life anecdotes to the dull rules and procedures. He'd been a cost accountant for years with the Shell Oil Company and he came prepared not only with a full understanding of the truth (cost-accounting formulas and structures) but with real-life examples. He helped us see how we could use the material in our own lives too. He wasn't just interested in pumping us full of data and formulas; we had the textbook for that. What he really wanted was to see us using cost accounting for some greater good in our lives and professions.

It's interesting that in the ancient Hebrew culture of the Old Testament, instruction followed along similar lines. William Barclay writes:

If Jewish religion had faltered, or altered, the Jews would have ceased to exist. First and foremost, the Jewish ideal of education is the ideal of holiness, of difference, of separation from all other peoples in order to belong to God. Their educational system was nothing less than the instrument by which their existence as a nation, and their fulfillment of their destiny, was ensured.[6]

In other words, the Jewish concept of education involved so much more than simply imparting knowledge. It was a concept deeply rooted in the idea of transmitting a culture of holiness and advancing a distinctive lifestyle. It is important to understand this concept because the Apostle Paul uses this same approach as he trains Timothy and Titus in ministry.

When Paul wrote to Timothy, his concept of "teaching" came from his Hebrew roots, not twentieth-century institutions. Paul was nearly demanding that these two men take an active approach in teaching their congregations. He wanted them to instill in the people a biblical knowledge as well as a lifestyle. What are children but members of our family "church"? Parents are mothers, fathers, and pastors to their offspring. Again, Paul's words to Timothy can also be addressed to us, especially those in 1 Timothy 1:5 (NIV):

The goal of this command is love, which comes from a pure heart and a good conscience and a sincere faith.

Paul is talking to Timothy about instruction, and in verse 5 he gives us his goal for teaching. Because of his rich Jewish background, Paul's educational goals aren't limited to the mastery of intellectual knowledge, but to the production of love, faith, and godliness in the lives of others. What a phenomenal goal for us parents—to produce love, faith, and godliness in our children through everyday teaching!

I believe we ought to share a joint concern with Paul. He was obviously concerned with more than conveying facts; he was supremely interested in how the truth manifested itself in believers' everyday lives. For Paul, a thing was truly learned when it was lived.

All of this tells you why Pam and I made it our goal to teach our children in a way that would help them with life. A little earlier in this chapter, I mentioned how we usually spent Saturdays. Zachary and I would mow the front lawn (or do some other household chore) and then we would always need a break. Typically, our break time was spent with a glass of iced tea for me and a cup of apple juice for Zachary. Sometimes, for a real treat, we'd have some Gatorade. We would get our drinks, sit in the shade, and just talk. These were wonderful instructional times for Zachary and me. I am a tall man, and when Zachary was smaller, these break times put us at face level—I sat down on the concrete walkway alongside him and we talked about anything and everything, from sports to school to life. It was my desire to communicate with Zachary and teach him (no matter how small the eventual lesson). It was also my goal to pour biblical teaching—with all naturalness—into our everyday conversations.

Another opportunity for this kind of instruction came every evening when Pam and I had devotions with our family. We would gather after dinner in our family room and, together as a family, we'd "study" something. Sometimes it was a children's object lesson, sometimes it was a Bible story, and sometimes we simply read Scripture and reflected upon God's message. We had some of the best discussions! What made those times precious was the non-threatening nature of the teaching we attempted. Pam and I would always try to link truth with life and communicate content and lifestyle. We would freely admit our mistakes in life, and we would spend time showing the children how God had worked within our daily routines.

The children felt free to ask questions and share. We prayed for each other and saw, together, how God answered our prayers. The twentieth-century model for education (transmission of information) wasn't sufficient for these special times. We were concerned with communicating our faith through real examples and in real time, using both our successes and our failures as primary illustrations.

Our goal was to touch the entire person, shaping beliefs, attitudes, values, and behaviors.

In order to enable our children, we parents must be willing to extend teaching beyond processing information. Such instruction involves urging, commanding, telling stories, setting examples, and becoming a role model. This kind of enabling requires our personal involvement to the extent that we're no longer expecting the church or school to do the fundamental job of conveying lifestyle to our children. Effective parental teaching, then, is bringing scriptural truth to bear on the everyday. It is taking time to sit and talk to our children. It is the extra five minutes at night, before bedtime, where encouragement takes place, where we ask meaningful questions and listen closely. It is being open to their needs and hearing them. It also means listening to their questions and being ready to help them find answers. Teaching is enabling our children to see our foundational values and motivations so they can build the structure of their own lives.[7]

ACTION-ROLE #3: ENCOURAGING

Our constant encouragement helps our children see their strengths and moves them forward in their dreams. I'm so happy that Pam has the gift of encouragement. It has been a sheer delight to see her work with our kids and give them just the right word at just the right time. She was especially helpful to our children during their school years. I can remember time after time when our children were discouraged or didn't trust God in certain situations. Pam was there, always offering reassuring thoughts, Bible stories, and praise.

One particular instance sticks in our son Zachary's mind. He was in high school and was under some pretty heavy pressure. He'd made a few poor decisions in his junior year, and yet he wanted to be accepted into a rather tough engineering school for college. He would have to get almost straight A's during the first semester of his senior year in order to qualify. From the first day, Pam believed in him and his ability. Zachary didn't believe in himself, but Pam did, and she kept encouraging him. It seemed as if every day Pam would develop a new method of encouragement with Zachary. Slowly he began believing in himself, and by the end of the first quarter, he had achieved those straight A's.

As the second quarter began, Pam continued her special encouraging words and actions. Zachary was working hard now, and by the end of the semester, Zachary had been accepted into the engineering school. It was obvious to all of us that Zachary had the talent and skill, but Pam's constant encouragement provided the extra incentive for him to excel.

I do not have such a gift. My ability to encourage our children had to be learned. I needed gentle reminders from God and Pam on a regular basis. So please don't worry if you are like me instead of Pam. If we move forward trusting God and listening to Him, we can develop the "encouragement muscle" and enable our children every day.

One of the greatest character studies in encouragement is the biblical Barnabas. What an interesting man! Along with numerous other acts of encouragement, he helped Paul establish his place among the disciples and helped pave the way for increased ministry in Jerusalem. In Acts 11 we find an example of the fruit of Barnabas' public ministry:

22b They sent Barnabas to Antioch.
23 When he arrived and saw the evidence of the grace of God, he was glad and encouraged them all to remain true to the Lord with all their hearts.
24 He was a good man, full of the Holy Spirit and faith, and a great number of people were brought to the Lord.
—Acts 11:22-24 (NIV)

Barnabas came alongside a new congregation, saw the evidence of God's grace, and encouraged the people to remain true with all their hearts. He so encouraged the congregation that many came to the Lord because of his life and exhortation. Who wouldn't want to join such a body of believers? Barnabas set the tone of a positive, encouraging church. Parents can do the same thing as they use encouragement to create positive families.

I must stop for a minute and give recognition to a world-class encourager. Pastor Gary Hardin, currently the senior pastor of Cornerstone Church in Ann Arbor, Michigan, is an encourager. Every Sunday Gary encourages his flock. Our praise band practiced on Wednesday evenings, and Gary would come by, put his arms around us and hug us, then tell us how much he appreciated our music ministry. Gary was our Barnabas. Don't you think we played hard and practiced hard knowing how Gary felt? He always finds time to encourage people, and his church is growing quickly because of his open, loving heart and quick-to-encourage mindset. Encouragement is contagious too. Gary's church is full of encouragers because he sets the pace. He is the role model, and people just naturally follow his fine example of encouraging others.

Perhaps Barnabas' greatest work of encouragement was with young John Mark. Acts 15 tells us the story:

> *36 Some time later Paul said to Barnabas, "Let us go back and visit the brothers in all the towns where we preached the word of the Lord and see how they are doing."*
> *37 Barnabas wanted to take John, also called Mark, with them,*
> *38 but Paul didn't think it wise to take him, because he had deserted them in Pamphylia and had not continued with them in the work.*
> *39 They had such a sharp disagreement that they parted company. Barnabas took Mark and sailed for Cyprus. . . .*
> —Acts 15:36-39 (NIV)

Paul was inflexible because he didn't see Mark as fit for service. In his mind, John Mark had failed (see Acts 13:13), and Paul thought he couldn't be trusted again. Yet Barnabas' love led him to hope for the best in Mark. In the above verses, Barnabas wouldn't give up and Paul wouldn't change, so they agreed to tackle different aspects of the work and part company. Later, and because of Barnabas' faith and encouragement, Mark proved so faithful that even the one who wasn't impressed later wrote and asked for him (2 Tim. 4:11). Such was the encouraging ministry of Barnabas.

If we look at the book of 1 Thessalonians, we see in chapter 5 a checklist where Paul gives some specific examples of how we can encourage others. Take your Bible and look at 1 Thessalonians 5:11-23 as you study the chart on pages 65 and 66. Perhaps you'll come up with your own practical applications of these encouraging verses.

Paul gives us parents plenty of encouragement in these verses as we take God's hand, trust Him, and begin to encourage our children. But we have other resources, too. Years ago I was impressed by the management teachings of Dr. Kenneth Blanchard. His books,

Verse 11	Build each other up. Point out a quality you appreciate in him or her.
Verse 12	Respect leaders. Look for ways to cooperate.
Verse 13	Hold leaders in highest regard. Hold back your next critical comment about those in positions of responsibility. Say "thank you" to your leaders for their efforts. Encourage them.
Verse 13	Live in peace. Search for ways to get along with and encourage others.
Verse 14	Warn the idle. Challenge (exhort) someone to join you in a project.
Verse 14	Encourage the timid. Encourage those who are timid by reminding them of God's promises.
Verse 14	Help the weak. Support those who are weak by loving them and praying for them.
Verse 14	Be patient. Think of a situation that tries your patience and plan ahead of time how you can stay calm.
Verse 15	Resist revenge. Instead of planning to get even with those who mistreat you, do good to them.
Verse 16	Be joyful. Remember that even in the midst of turmoil, God is in control.
Verse 17	Pray continually. God is always with you—talk to Him and encourage others to talk to Him as well.

Verse 18	Give thanks. Make a list of all the gifts God has given you, giving thanks for each one. Encourage others to do the same and pray together in thanksgiving.
Verse 19	Do not put out the Spirit's fire. Cooperate with the Spirit the next time He prompts you to participate in a Christian meeting, or encourage a friend or loved one.
Verse 20	Do not treat prophecies with contempt. Receive God's word from those who speak for Him. Take time to encourage them as well. They need to hear how their preaching has positively affected your life.
Verse 22	Avoid every kind of evil. Avoid situations where you will be drawn into temptation. Help others be accountable as well with chosen positive words.
Verse 23	Count on God's constant help. Realize that the Christian life is to be lived not in our own strength but through God's power. Realize too that encouraging others comes from God's power not our own strength.[8]

like *The One-Minute Manager*, overflow with practical principles on leadership and people development. He presents a concept called "one-minute praisings." I've taken the liberty to modify his ideas a bit for use by us parents. One-minute praising works well when you:

• *Tell children up front that you're going to let them know how they're doing.* Would you enjoy bowling if there were a bed sheet hanging in front of the pins so you couldn't see how many pins you knocked down? Of course not. We need to know how many pins we knocked down so we'll know how well, or in what direction, we need to roll the ball to score higher. Now, imagine someone standing next to the bed sheet, holding up his fingers to indicate how many pins you knocked down. A little better, right? Finally, we have the encouraging parent. He or she would remove the sheet so the children could have immediate feedback. On top of that, the encouraging parent would be standing on the sidelines giving verbal praise and a "high five" for rolling the ball so well. This analogy points out the importance of feedback, both good and bad. The encouraging parent prepares children for feedback by telling them that they will be receiving it regularly.

• *Praise your children immediately.* The longer the time span between an achievement and praise for the achievement, the less effective is the praise. So . . . don't wait!

• *Tell your children what they did right—and be specific.* Most parents concentrate on what their children are doing wrong. Encouraging parents try to catch their children doing something right. There is a big difference. By receiving rewards for positive, productive behavior, children will learn quickly what is acceptable behavior and what behavior results in praise. Even busy parents understand that praise and encouragement are necessary every day. The important thing to remember is to "catch them doing things right."

• *Tell your children how good you feel about what they did right.* And tell them how it helps the family, themselves, and other people. The encouraging parent feels good about children doing things right and expresses those feelings sincerely and consistently. Children appreciate this—they receive a warm feeling every time Mom or Dad looks them straight in the eye to express appreciation and recognition for a job well done.

• *Stop for a moment of silence.* Just let them drink in how good you feel. Three seconds of a silent, thoughtful nod are worth twice as much as a twenty-second "jibber jabber" expression of thanks. Silence is powerful.

• *Encourage them to do more of the same.* If children are on the right track, let them know that. Encourage them to repeat excellent behavior. They will.

• *Give them a big hug.* Do this in a way that makes it clear you support their success. Touch is very powerful. It tells kids you care enough about them to make warm contact. Be cautious of personal space, however, and always make the touch sincere and non-threatening.[9]

Extending encouragement enables our children. It requires expressing positive feedback and warmly congratulating behavior. It means finding them doing things right instead of focusing on what they've done wrong. The great thing is that any one of us can be an encourager in our family, if we apply TRUST and take the initiative to look for the opportunities.

THINK AND TALK ABOUT IT

1. Who among the people you know do you think will receive the greatest rewards in heaven?
2. What three acts can you do today in service to your children?
3. What responsibility do you have as parents to teach your children?
4. How can you start today to encourage your children?

Notes

1 Edythe Draper, *Draper's Book of Quotations*, #8302.

2 William Raspberry, quoted in "Festival Quarterly," (Carol Stream, IL: Christianity Today, Inc.), Vol. 30, no. 5

3 *Strong's Dictionary*, Bible Explorer, version 2

4 John Ortberg, *Leadership Journal* (Carol Stream, IL: Christianity Today, Inc.), Vol. 14, No. 3.

5 Edythe Draper, *Draper's Book of Quotations*, #2993.

6 William Barclay, *Educational Ideals in the Ancient World* (Grand Rapids, MI: Baker Book House), 125.

7 The material for this section was taken from a number of sources. Primary sources included *Vine's Complete Expository Dictionary of Old and New Testament Words* and *The Teacher's Commentary*.

8 Portions of this table are taken from *The Life Application Bible* Notes (Wheaton, IL: Tyndale House Publishers).

9 Portions taken from Ken Blanchard, *The One-Minute Manager*.

Chapter 4

TRUSTING ENOUGH TO PREPARE

HAVE YOU EVER WATCHED A COOKING SHOW ON TV? Not only do you discover some wonderful new recipes, you witness in living color the miracle of advanced preparation. In the typical show, the cook approaches a stovetop covered with pans and kettles already cooking their savory ingredients. She—let's call her Julia—reaches for ingredients that are already measured. The pan already has just enough oil in it for whatever is to be sauteed or fried.

Once Julia has mixed the premeasured, sorted, and sifted ingredients together they're placed in a baking dish and swept rather elegantly into just the right-sized baking dish. It's all then hoisted into a gleaming preheated oven.

Then—much to our surprise—the second door of the oven swings open and . . . *voila!* We feast our eyes on a delectable, already-cooked version of the recipe. Julia and her host grab a napkin, lift their forks, and . . .

Well, you get the picture. Pure perfection—all in thirty minutes or less.

TAKE TIME TO PREPARE

Unfortunately, rearing children isn't a cooking show. If it were, it would certainly take on a whole new look. Just think: whatever we wanted would be there, right in front of us, already measured and sifted. Need a little discipline? Well, right at our elbow is one premeasured cupful. Need to teach the children about telling the truth? Right here at our fingertips is just the right lesson. Need a stirring message to encourage good grades and better study habits? It comes already prepared, straight from the heart.

In reality, when our children come to ask us a burning question or present some startling news, it's usually the worst time for us, and what we need at the moment is hardly at our fingertips. Nor do we have a smiling host ready to hand it to us. We'll need to dig around a bit, fishing for the right response while taking time away from an already late project. No, parenting isn't a cooking show. Parenting is hard work, and it definitely requires preparation.

"Prepare" means to put in order or to organize. We prepare to go on vacation, or we prepare for a visit from Aunt Alice. In so doing, we put things in order or organize them so we'll be ready for any eventuality in advance. It means taking the time to *anticipate what is going to happen* as well as being ready to meet new challenges on the spur of the moment.

As best we could, Pam and I frequently communicated with our kids about drugs, premarital sex, and other issues. We knew it was our responsibility to prepare them for the time when they would be faced with making quick decisions on their own. The time to have an answer about drugs is *before* someone offers them to you at a school party; the time to have an answer for a boyfriend or girlfriend isn't in the heat of the moment, but during a "preparatory" conversation or in a calm environment.

We took time to discuss these matters in order to prepare our children for the inevitable pressure times. We wanted them to know all the facts. We wanted them to be ready with a decision. We wanted them to know God's Word on the subject, and we wanted the opportunity to pray with them. We prayed for God's protection and wisdom right alongside our children. And in private, as a couple, we prayed that God would bring to mind what we had discussed.

And we tried to remember the power of frequency. As parents we found that we needed to continue these dialogues as the subjects presented themselves. It wasn't enough to cover a sensitive subject simply one time; we had to reintroduce the subjects, reinforce the teachings, continue the dialogues. We accomplished this by seizing on everyday events as the discussion starters. We tried not to set up formal lecture times; rather, we simply let daily events usher in the topics. It was fun, it was challenging, and we believe it paid off.

Preparation of ourselves first, and then our children, is crucial if we are to TRUST enough to parent. Let's examine an encounter between David and Solomon to see the importance of preparation from the biblical perspective.

6 Then he called for his son Solomon and charged him to build a house for the LORD, the God of Israel.

7 David said to Solomon: "My son, I had it in my heart to build a house for the Name of the LORD my God.

8 But this word of the LORD came to me: 'You have shed much blood and have fought many wars. You are not to build a house for my Name, because you have shed much blood on the earth in my sight.

9 But you will have a son who will be a man of peace and rest, and I will give him rest from all his enemies on every side. His name will be Solomon, and I will grant Israel peace and quiet during his reign.

10 He is the one who will build a house for my Name. He will be my son, and I will be his father. And I will establish the throne of his kingdom over Israel forever.

11 "Now, my son, the LORD be with you, and may you have success and build the house of the LORD your God, as he said you would.

12 May the LORD give you discretion and understanding when he puts you in command over Israel, so that you may keep the law of the LORD your God.

13 Then you will have success if you are careful to observe the decrees and laws that the LORD gave Moses for Israel. Be strong and courageous. Don't be afraid or discouraged.

14 "I have taken great pains to provide for the temple of the LORD a hundred thousand talents of gold, a million talents of silver, quantities of bronze and iron too great to be weighed, and wood and stone. And you may add to them.

15 You have many workmen: stonecutters, masons and carpenters, as well as men skilled in every kind of work

16 in gold and silver, bronze and iron—craftsmen beyond number. Now begin the work, and the LORD be with you."

—1 Chronicles 22:6-16 (NIV)

Seek the Lord

David was passing along to Solomon the important and highly emotional (for David) task of building the temple. In this conversation, David is preparing Solomon for the task and also showing him the preparations that were already accomplished. In these Scriptures, David provides some truths that will help us as we seek to prepare our children.

In verses 7 through 10, it becomes obvious that David had spent considerable time with the Lord concerning this issue of temple building. David had heard from the Lord that he wouldn't be able to build the temple, but his son, a man of peace (Solomon, whose name in Hebrew, *Shalom*, means peace), would have that responsibility. At this point in his life David was close to death, and he was now preparing his son to take charge of a responsibility that David had thought would be his. But it wasn't to be; instead, Solomon would need preparation for the task.

So David charges his son with the responsibility to build the house for the Lord. In verses 11 and 12, David asks that the Lord be with Solomon and he asks the Lord for prosperity, wisdom, and understanding. What a great model for us as we move to preparing our children! By asking that the Lord be with Solomon, David is seeking a blessing from the Lord. He is saying, "Lord, my desire is for You to be with my son, that he will never depart from You."

First, David asks for *success*, or *prosperity*. He knows that Solomon will need to overcome numerous hurdles and obstacles in order to prosper in the construction work. He takes the time to ask God specifically for guidance in his son's life. The Hebrew root word for "prosperity" means "to accomplish satisfactorily what is intended." Real prosperity results from the work of God in those who seek Him with all their heart. David was a man after God's own heart, and he knew what a lifetime spent seeking God would mean to Solomon. He wanted Solomon to stay on track, not only for the temple project, but also for a lifetime of joy and fulfillment.

Second, David asks for *wisdom*. The Hebrew word is *sakal*, and it refers to an intelligent knowledge of the reason. This is the process of *thinking through a complex arrangement of thoughts*, resulting in wise dealings and use of practical common sense.

Wouldn't a basis of practical common sense and knowledge—straight from our desire to seek the Lord—be a wonderful concept to help prepare our children for success in life? Another meaning of the verb *sakal* is "to have insight or comprehension." The person who would boast of anything should boast that he has insight into, and knows the Lord (see Jeremiah 9:23-24). David shows great wisdom as he prepares Solomon by seeking God and asking wisdom for his son.

Third, David asks God to give his son *understanding*. This word means "discernment." Its most common usage has to do with "discerning between" two things. David was preparing his son to discern between good and evil. In many of our discussions with our children, we prayed for their discernment of good and evil, of right and wrong behaviors. We talked and prayed and sought after God. We especially asked for discernment when our kids entered those unavoidable pressure situations.

Study His Word

In preparing our children, it's not only important to seek God, but also to immerse ourselves in His Word. As a family we enjoyed devotions almost every night. This time together gave us a chance to study the Bible and opened doors to significant conversations with our children. Many times the questions from our children were much more challenging than the discussion questions in our Bible study guide. And that's a good thing! The Book of 2 Timothy gives us more insight into this second principle of preparation.

1 In the presence of God and of Christ Jesus, who will judge the living and the dead, and in view of his appearing and his kingdom, I give you this charge:
2 Preach the Word; be prepared in season and out of season; correct, rebuke and encourage—with great patience and careful instruction.
3 For the time will come when men will not put up with sound doctrine. Instead, to suit their own desires, they will gather around them a great number of teachers to say what their itching ears want to hear.
4 They will turn their ears away from the truth and turn

aside to myths.
—2 Timothy 4:1-4 (NIV)

As Paul comes to the end of this letter, he wants to challenge Timothy regarding his church members. I believe Paul's words have great meaning to those of us who are parents, as well. His first lesson for Timothy (and parents) is to *be urgent.*

> *The teachers [parents] who really get their message across are those who have the note of earnestness in their voice. Spurgeon had a real admiration for Martineau, who was a Unitarian and therefore denied the divinity of Jesus Christ that Spurgeon believed in with passionate intensity. Someone once said to Spurgeon: "How can you possibly admire Martineau? You don't believe what he preaches." "No," said Spurgeon, "but he does." Any man with the note of urgency in his voice demands, and will receive, a hearing from other men.[1]*

Urgency is important because we don't know how long we have to prepare our children before they will need help. We as parents must take a full measure of every opportunity to share God's Word.

The second lesson from this passage is that parents, when they are delivering God's Word, must *be persistent.* Roberto C. Goizueta rose from the ranks to become president of the Coca-Cola Company, one of the world's largest business enterprises. One of his favorite sayings is from the Japanese writer Xishima: "To know and not to act isn't yet to know." He has made that a guiding principle of his life. His advice to young managers is: "Do the best you can and a little bit more. The rest will take care of itself."[2] That is sound advice for parents. FEAR instead of TRUST often grips us, and we don't do the best we can in situations with our children. As we teach God's Word, we should be persistent and do the best we can in every situation. If we do, we will see significant differences in our children's lives.

Third, preparing our children with God's Word should foster conviction. We as parents *must seek to convict* when we teach our children—and our children will be convicted when they encounter tempting situations and draw upon our teaching for support.

The same is true for rebuking, for Paul is telling Timothy to be strong with his people. We parents, likewise, must *be strong* with our children, and rebuking (we will see this in a later chapter on discipline) is part of our charge. In our relationships with our children, a word of warning and rebuke would often save them from many perils. It must be spoken without inflicting guilt or from a "moral judgment" platform. Nevertheless, the right words from Scripture must be spoken when they need to be spoken.

We must *exhort*. No rebuke should ever drive our children into discouragement. Such negativity will take the hope right out of them. So along with every rebuke should come a word of encouragement or exhortation.

Paul gives the reason for all this in verses 3 and 4. He tells Timothy, "For there will come a time . . . ." Yes, it will be a time when your children and my children are faced with terrible temptations and obstacles. It is our job, according to Paul, to preach the Word so when they stumble on these things, when they are tempted, or when they want their "ears tickled," they will have a solid base of wisdom to discern what they should do—and the character to follow through with action.

Seeking to teach God's Word, then, involves:

- Urgency (there is no time like the present)
- Persistence (never stop)
- Conviction (be passionate, be bold)
- Rebuking (tell it like it is)
- Exhorting (find them doing things right)

Follow the Spirit

As we prepare our children, we must make certain the Holy Spirit leads us. The Spirit must lead us as parents, and we must transfer to our children their need to be led by the Spirit as well.

16 So I say, live by the Spirit, and you will not gratify the desires of the sinful nature.
17 For the sinful nature desires what is contrary to the Spirit, and the Spirit what is contrary to the sinful nature.

They are in conflict with each other, so that you don't do
what you want.
18 But if you are led by the Spirit, you are not under law.
—Galatians 5:16-18 (NIV)

Here Paul is contrasting two forces—the Holy Spirit and the spirit of evil. He's saying, "You need to make wise choices." If we don't allow ourselves to be led by the Holy Spirit, we leave ourselves open to making lousy choices. In addition, if we try to be led by the Holy Spirit on our own strength, we will fail as well. Our will and strength must be given over to the Spirit. He is stronger and will prevail over evil; however, it is up to us to allow Him to lead us.

Paul also speaks of a freedom when the Spirit leads us. Either terrible desires will trap us, or we can be free in the Spirit. We as parents need to demonstrate that kind of freedom to our children and help them see the difference between a life of being led by the Spirit and a life of bondage to things of the world. We must help them see as we seek and teach, that the Holy Spirit will lead us to the best decisions in the midst of everyday spiritual battles.

Zachary and I used to play football together. We'd developed certain rules, and we created this little game we played in our backyard. We had a great time being silly while playing hard, but the backyard still had an old swing set in it, blocking off part of our playing field. When we finally decided to take it out—it had been anchored in concrete with pipes—we left the pipes in the ground. They were buried, seemingly well below the surface.

You probably know what's coming. One afternoon I kicked off to Zachary and the kick went straight up. He had to run forward and dive for the ball. To my horror, he dove right where the swing set had been, and his knee smashed directly into the pipe that was fixed in concrete. I could hardly believe my eyes as I surveyed the damage to his knee; I saw nothing but blood, ligament, and bone.

I ran into the house, and had Pam quickly call our doctor. At the same time, I ran back outside with towels to press against the gash and stop the bleeding. What was my ten-year-old son doing? He was praying. He was saying, "Help me, Jesus; help me, Jesus" repeatedly. I was a basket case, and my son was a spiritual warrior evoking the power of Jesus.

Had he been prepared? I like to think he was. He allowed the Holy Spirit to direct him to pray and seek God in spite of great pain and a terrible looking gash in his knee. Thankfully, he sustained no permanent damage, just a long scar. However, I will never forget his seeking God that afternoon. We had prepared him to call upon the Lord, and the Spirit had prompted him to look not at his frightful circumstance but instead at the Great Physician. Romans 15:13 sums it all up for me: "Now may the God of hope fill you with all joy and peace in believing, that you may abound in hope by the power of His Holy Spirit" (NASB).

BE SURE TO EQUIP

I played city-league basketball as a youngster, but our town hadn't budgeted funds for our uniforms. We had shirts but no matching shorts. One of my classmate's fathers took it upon himself to provide those shorts for us. I still remember the day when we all trotted down to the local sporting goods store to outfit ourselves in brand new (and matching!) basketball shorts. What a thrill the first time we wore our uniforms! We were so happy to look like a real team.

In similar fashion, we need to enable our children by equipping them for the Kingdom team. We need to give them an abundance of tools they can use whenever they need them. This will keep them growing strong in the faith. In a sense, we parents serve as the supply sergeants for our children, building up the inventory of biblical tools they need to face the world. I'd like to suggest three tools that are absolutely necessary as we equip our children. They are the tools of faith, prayer, and submission.

The Tool of Faith

We spent a whole chapter talking about trust and faith, so I won't duplicate that here. Suffice it to say that this tool does have, like a good Swiss army knife, some extra "gadgets" that I believe we should pull out and examine:

• *The Blade of Salvation.* Do lead your children to faith in Christ! What we have shared to this point is based upon your children knowing Christ as their savior. The power of parents to TRUST enough includes children who have been taught the saving message of Christ. Franz Gillparzer, the great Austrian poet, once wrote, "Greatness is dangerous. One thing alone can bring happiness here on earth, and that is peace within us and a heart that knows no guilt."[3] The blade of salvation is the only thing that can bring our children peace, true happiness, and no guilt. Isaiah 32:17 says, "The fruit of righteousness will be peace; the effect of righteousness will be quietness and confidence forever." Whatever it takes, make certain you know the Savior and that you are equipping your children to trust Him as well.

The Blade of Protection. As we equip our children in the midst of TRUSTING enough to parent, let's not forget that faith itself will protect our children. Hebrews 10:22 (NIV) says,

Let us draw near to God with a sincere heart in full assurance of faith, having our hearts sprinkled to cleanse us from a guilty conscience and having our bodies washed with pure water. Let us hold unswervingly to the hope we profess, for he who promised is faithful.

What a promise for our children! To be told to draw near to God with a heart of faith. Do you see the protection? The Hebrews, when they read this passage, must have been absolutely blown away. Everything in Judaism told them "separate yourselves" from what might be either contaminating or too holy. This verse, however, tells them to "draw near."

Our children may feel like those Israelites. They may feel lonely, insecure, ugly, unwanted, and generally lousy. However, as we TRUST enough to parent and begin equipping them with faith, they will feel the warm invitation of this Scripture to draw near and be washed by God's pure water of love and forgiveness. Draw near and I will rid you of that guilty conscience, says God. Draw near, for the hope is here, if you are faithful. Draw near to Me—the loving, living God.

The Blade of Belief. Every day we need to TRUST enough to encourage belief. We can model for our children the lifestyle that is based upon belief and not deception or mistrust. Our trust resides in God and God alone, and our behavior, when modeled for our children, will give them the strong blade of belief. After all, each and every day they will encounter reasons for unbelief.

It has been said that only man comprehends what he can't see and believes what he can't comprehend. Much of what we comprehend we can't see: atoms, germs, love, hate, loyalty, sacrifice. He who lives by sight lives poorly indeed. Faith is learning to live by insight rather than by sight.[4]

The Tool of Prayer

Equipping our children also means praying with them and outfitting them with the tool of prayer in their own lives. Early in their lives children can learn to appreciate praying as they watch their parents taking everything to the Lord. Our family devotional times always ended in prayer. When Zachary was small (not quite two), he had three nightly prayer requests. He prayed for our next-door neighbor, the mail carrier, and his grandfather. These three men had something in common—they all smoked, and for some reason Zachary took it upon himself to pray for them. One weekend, his grandfather got him on the telephone and asked him what he was doing. "I pray that you no smoke anymore" was Zachary's reply. Without delay my father, who had smoked for over fifty years, quit cold turkey. He has not had another cigarette to this day, almost nineteen years later. Zachary appreciates the power of prayer!

Warren Wiersbe in his book, *Be Complete*,[5] says that in our prayer time with our children, we should point them into the direction of (1) spiritual intelligence (*discerning* God's will), (2) practical obedience (committing to *doing* God's will), and (3) moral excellence (*maintaining a lifestyle* of seeking and obeying God). In this regard, have you noticed how convicting it can be to pray for wisdom and obedience? One leads to another; as we learn more, we want to obey more. The more we obey, the more we want to learn. The goal is to live the way God wants us to live, and it is only through prayer that we can achieve the goal for our children and ourselves.

Through prayer we can help our children gain knowledge of God, understand obedience to God, and develop a positive moral character. Only through prayer will there be conviction, personal reflection, and answers from heaven.

We, as parents, need to take the lead and help our children not only see the benefits of prayer (intellectual decision), but actively pray together so they can see the answers to prayer (experiential decision). One of the methods we used was a simple prayer journal. We could record our prayers and keep track of how God answered them. This helped us not only realize the victory of answered prayers, but also helped us develop patience as we waited for God's response (which was sometimes: "Wait!"). It's amazing to see how God answers our children's prayers and how they can learn about God's power and patience through prayer.

The Tool of Submission

One day I faced the distressing prospect of coming home and telling my family that I'd been laid off from my job. It was the first time it had happened to me. We had just moved to accommodate this job, we loved the house and the area, and we thought we had settled in. How wrong we were!

So I came home and told my wife the news first. Then we told the children. We didn't know exactly what to do; we were all a little panicked and crying. Zachary then prayed, "Lord, for every door you close, you open a window." That became our rallying cry for the next several weeks as God took us on an unexpected journey to not only a new job, but a new home, a new state, and a completely new climate. Helen Keller said, "When one door of happiness closes, another opens; but often we look so long at the closed door that we don't see the one which has been opened for us."[6] Zachary's prayer helped us look away from the closed door and look at open doors. One of those open doors was simply this: submission to God's will. We had spent countless hours in Bible study and prayer, and they paid off that day when Zachary gave us his advice to look for an open window. He had learned, at a young age, the power of surrender. Have you learned this lesson yet?

To help us remove any obstacles that might be in the way, we need to take inventory of two aspects of surrender: how we surrender to God and how we surrender our "self."

•*Surrendering to God.* One night, Jacob, a patriarch of the Old Testament, learned a valuable lesson. This particular story captures the basics of surrendering everything to God. We may have a wrestling match with an angel, or we might just wrestle with ourselves, but we will not win the battle until we learn to surrender ourselves to God.

22 That night Jacob got up and took his two wives, his two maidservants and his eleven sons and crossed the ford of the Jabbok.

23 After he had sent them across the stream, he sent over all his possessions.

24 So Jacob was left alone, and a man wrestled with him till daybreak.

25 When the man saw that he couldn't overpower him, he touched the socket of Jacob's hip so that his hip was wrenched as he wrestled with the man.

26 Then the man said, "Let me go, for it is daybreak." But Jacob replied, "I will not let you go unless you bless me."

27 The man asked him, "What is your name?" "Jacob," he answered.

28 Then the man said, "Your name will no longer be Jacob, but Israel, because you have struggled with God and with men and have overcome."

29 Jacob said, "Please tell me your name." But he replied, "Why do you ask my name?" Then he blessed him there.

30 So Jacob called the place Peniel, saying, "It is because I saw God face to face, and yet my life was spared."

31 The sun rose above him as he passed Peniel, and he was limping because of his hip.

32 Therefore to this day the Israelites don't eat the tendon attached to the socket of the hip, because the socket of Jacob's hip was touched near the tendon.

—Genesis 32:22-32 (NIV)

Jacob was about to confront something that had probably haunted him for years—he was going to see his brother Esau. Remember that Jacob had schemed and taken away Esau's birthright (Gen. 25:33) and his blessing (Gen. 27:27-40). Now he was going to see Esau for the first time in twenty years. He's frantic. Nevertheless, much to his credit, he prays.

How well do we as parents meet obstacles that are difficult to handle? We see our children misbehave, or we see them in painful situations. Generally, our first reaction is frantic. We run around grumbling or complaining, crying or yelling, fearful of the outcome.

Parents who TRUST enough to parent, however, are like Jacob. They stop the erratic behavior of their own and commit the situation to prayer and trust. Prayer always comes before trusting. Jacob showed how he had matured as a man of God as he surrendered the upcoming situation to God's control.

In verse 26, Jacob is persistent in his wrestling match with God. He knows with whom he's wrestling, and he will not stop until he receives a blessing. God likes our persistence, and He wants to bless us. Jacob stayed with it; he didn't surrender to vain thoughts or FEAR. He kept "wrestling," and he gained the divine approval for which he was looking.

Sometimes submission to God comes with a price. In Jacob's case (see verse 31), it was lameness. He had just received his greatest victory, and the angel makes it clear that Jacob will never forget that victory. During his greatest triumph, Jacob is also given a humble reminder, much like Paul's "thorn in the flesh." Every day, for the rest of his life, Jacob would remember that moment of surrender. His broken hip would always remind him, and the ache and pain would serve him well.

• *Letting Go of Self.* A man once boasted that he was self-made. Joseph Parker replied, "That relieves the Lord of an awful responsibility."[7] In our society, we see a lot of "self" promotion. It doesn't matter what direction we turn in the media—TV, books, magazines, or newspapers—somebody or some company is calling us to "self express" or trumpeting the benefits of "I did it my way."

If we as parents want to TRUST and release, then the act of submitting ourselves is the key. This frees us to make corrections in our parenting skills as well as releasing our children to excel. We all need to self-criticize our parenting behavior and skill. Only parents who have made a firm commitment to surrendering themselves will put their egos on the shelf for a time and allow for a change in direction or method. Being surrendered means being open and ready to embrace new insights and lessons from God and others.

We also need to let go of our selves as we view our children's growth and success—often in fields or endeavors that are different from what we would choose for ourselves. I remember when I played Little League baseball. One boy on the team (nicknamed Mouse for his size) obviously didn't want to be there. He was only on the team because his dad wanted him there. At practice he would cry, and when he rarely played, he was so nervous that he struck out or bungled easy plays. He was miserable, and, looking back, I am sure his father was miserable as well.

So why did Dad force Mouse to play? It's because Dad wasn't willing to let go of self and rejoice in whatever his son chose to do as a hobby. In our house, our children chose different routes than we had pursued. Jennifer loved acting and singing on stage—her mother dreads public speaking and being up front. Zachary loved music and computers—my passion was sports. But we made a decision early in our child-rearing adventure that we would step aside and heartily support what our children wanted to do as opposed to what we wanted them to do. We became their loudest cheerleaders and we all won in the end. We surrendered self and TRUSTED God for the rest.

THINK AND TALK ABOUT IT

1. Although severely tested and persecuted, Paul and Silas held onto their faith and their joy; how do you think you would hold up under such extraordinary pressure? Why?
2. What are some personal miracles that you could share with your children that demonstrate submitting to God's will?
3. What one thing could you do today to equip your children to have more faith? Prayer? An attitude of submission?
4. What is one step toward surrendering your life to God? What is holding you back?

Notes

1 William Barclay, *Daily Study Bible-New Testament* (Louisville, KY: Westminster John Knox Press, 1975), Bible Explorer, Version 2.

2 Robert C. Shannon, *1000 Windows* (Cincinnati: Standard Publishing Company, 1997).

3 Ibid.

4 Ibid.

5 Warren Wiersbe, *Be Complete* (Colorado Springs: Chariot Victor Publishing, 1989).

6 *Holman Bible Dictionary* (Nashville: Holman Bible Publishers, 1991) in QuickVerse 5.0.

7 Robert C. Shannon, *1000 Windows*.

Chapter 5

TRUSTING ENOUGH TO LOVE

THINK OF ALL THE TIME WE SPEND SEARCHING for true love. Growing up, our innocent giggling with the opposite sex transforms into dating. When we find the "right one" we may then become engaged and enter marriage. Even as we get to know each other over the years, we're still on our quest for the best that love can be in our lives. Then children are placed into our hands, and we are to love them perfectly—and make a loving family. Can we do it?

Writer Patrick Morley says, "Love is the glue that holds us together and the oil that keeps us from rubbing each other the wrong way."[1] Yet TRUST and FEAR collide within many of us as we enter the love relationship of parenting our children. It's not as easy as it sounds just to "love them through it" as the realities, the tough choices, and the all-consuming demands of parenting begin to fall with full weight upon our shoulders.

But here's the good news: we can love our children with our whole hearts, and that love can shape them into the most beautiful creatures on earth. How do we do it? I can only answer from my own experience. As we came to know our children, Pam and I discovered that in order to fully love them we needed to help them know they were important, help them feel thoroughly special, and lead them to understand the precious value of failure in their spiritual growth.

CHILD, YOU ARE IMPORTANT!

Steven Spielberg's mother, Leah Adler, understood what it meant to make her now-famous son feel important. "I listened to what he said, took whatever he wanted to do seriously, and always made him feel important. Like the time the adolescent film maker was directing a big scene and wanted to create an explosion in my kitchen. He prompted me on cue to hurl cans of cherries in the air. The juice never came out of the wood. But it never occurred to me not to do it."[2]

So what does it mean to make your children feel important? I think the Bible speaks clearly on *why* they are important, so we will start our journey there. The point is, God says they are wonderfully made. Pam and I constantly repeated that message to our children, a truth that resounds in the words of Psalm 139. Here's how Eugene Peterson conveys it in his excellent Bible paraphrase:

Oh yes, you shaped me first inside, then out; you formed me in my mother's womb.
I thank you, High God—you're breathtaking! Body and soul, I am marvelously made! I worship in adoration— what a creation!
You know me inside and out, you know every bone in my body;
You know exactly how I was made, bit by bit, how I was sculpted from nothing into something.
Like an open book, you watched me grow from conception to birth; all stages of my life were spread out before you,
The days of my life all prepared before I'd even lived one day.
—Psalm 139:14-16 (TM)

Beverly LaHaye once wrote, "There is no one else in the world like your child. He is literally one of a kind. His particular combination of genes has never before existed and never will exist again. His label can read, 'An original created by God.'"[3] Our children are unique designer creations, each labeled with the divine logo. They are shaped by God, watched by God, prepared by God, and given a plan for their lives.

You Shaped Me

Our children are important because a loving God individually shaped each one from the moment of conception. Pam spent hours

praying for our children before they were born. She would sit silent-
ly and talk to God about our children. All that time, during the nine
months of pregnancy, God was shaping, forming, and creating a
new person—a special person just for us. Nobody else would look,
act, or be the same as Jennifer or Zachary. They are unique individuals who share common genes but are still so different. They
have some mannerisms that are similar; some are totally particular
to them. God shaped them.

The theme of verses 13-18 is declared in verse 14. The Lord created (or shaped) the writer in his mother's womb. The language is
figurative in the King James Version; "creating and knitting" describe
God's sovereign custody over the natural processes of reproduction.
This fact prompted David to break forth in praise over the thought
of how marvelously he had been made. Even David's simple knowledge of the miracle of the human body led him to awe and wonder. Every time I look at our children, I am amazed. I remember
when Zachary was born, and I just stared at his little fingers, in awe
of what God had created.

(Now, Dear Friend, I am not saying that babies never come to
us with deformities or that they always survive the birth process.
Some of you are grieving for children who lived far too briefly or
who could not survive their physical complications. My heart goes
out to you. I am saying here that God is the One behind life itself,
and this makes every life priceless in value. His purposes in allowing an imperfect world, where so much suffering pierces our hearts,
will someday be understood. Could it be that when all of life is
restored to glory at the end of time [see Rom. 8:18-30], our little
loved ones will finally be revealed in all the beauty of their inno-
cence? For any creature fully loved and restored by God can be
nothing but perfectly beautiful and whole.)

David realizes, too, that in the womb he was woven together
("embroidered" and "knit," likely referring to his veins and arteries).
When he was being formed in the womb, he was as remote to the
human eye as the lower part of the earth. However, God saw every
detail. What is even more unbelievable, God prerecorded all the
days of the psalmist before he was even born. God marvelously
planned David's life.

TRUSTING enough to love means that we as parents need to

help our children understand how important they are, simply because of the profound fact that the Creator of the Universe has also created them. We can help them recognize that God Himself made all of us. When they think they should have been created one way or another, or more like someone else than themselves, we need to jump in and help them fully understand that God in heaven shaped them exactly the way He wanted them. And besides being shaped, our children are so important to God that they are "watched" by Him.

You Watched Me

Our children can't escape God's loving sight. There is no place in the entire universe where He is not present, watching.

> *Is there anyplace I can go to avoid your Spirit? To be out of your sight?*
> *If I climb to the sky, you're there! If I go underground, you're there!*
> *If I flew on morning's wings to the far western horizon, You'd find me in a minute—you're already there waiting!*
> *Then I said to myself, "Oh, he even sees me in the dark! At night, I'm immersed in the light!"*
> *It's a fact: darkness isn't dark to you; night and day, darkness and light, they're all the same to you.*
> —Psalm 139:7-12 (TM)

David tells us that when we go somewhere (either mentally or physically), God is already there waiting for us. What a concept to explain to our children—you are so important that wherever you go God has already beaten you to the spot! We're so fearfully and wonderfully made by God that He "never leaves us or forsakes us." We are so important to God that He is not only with us, He is *within* us. He accompanies us everywhere. That is how important we are.

I went to a convention once where Prime Minister Margaret Thatcher of Britain was the featured guest speaker. As we all waited in great anticipation for her, suddenly the composition of the audience changed. Looking around, I noticed many men and women with earphones—small, discrete devices that plugged into one ear and had a small line running inside their jackets. Once the prime minister appeared, these people formed a ring around the area where she was standing and speaking. They were obviously secret service personnel. They went everywhere with her, and their purpose was protection from any enemy who wanted to do her harm.

God is like those agents with us. He surrounds us with His protection. We might not be able to see Him, but when we encounter an enemy, He is there ready to help us. In fact, He is there before we are.

This presence of God is the absolute closeness of love. This should bring us to a feeling of comfort and rest. We are important to God. He wants us to have comfort and rest, so He takes the time to watch and protect us. Parents who TRUST enough to love teach their children that they are important: shaped and immersed in divine love.

You Prepared Me

Let's look at the end of David's psalm:

> *Investigate my life, O God, find out everything about me;*
> *Cross-examine and test me, get a clear picture of what I'm about;*
> *See for yourself whether I've done anything wrong—then guide me on the road to eternal life.*
> —Psalm 139:23-24 (TM)

The end of verse 24 in the King James Version reads, "lead me in the way everlasting." Verse 16 in the same translation reads, "Thine eyes did see my substance, yet being unperfect; and in thy book all my members were written, which in continuance were fashioned, when as yet there was none of them." These two verses show us how God has prepared us and continues to prepare us for a life dedicated to Him.

God is leading us, and before He can lead us, He must "fashion" us. The word used for "fashion" here is *yatsar*, and it carries with it the image of a potter squeezing his clay into shape. David is asking God to prepare him, to fashion him into what He wants him to be.

The Jews celebrate preparation day, the sixth day of the week used for preparing life's necessities in order to avoid working on the seventh day. The orthodox take care of everything on that sixth day—meals, chores, and spiritual purifications included. They "prepare" for the holiest day of the week. God, in a similar way, is preparing our children. They are important to Him, and He so loves His creatures, that He will take the time to prepare them for whatever plan He has for them.

And God stirs the hearts of our children to do many things. We parents must love them enough—TRUST enough—to help them recognize God's stirrings in their hearts and to follow those directives. He is preparing them and we need to help them, love them enough to pave the way for them.

You Gave Me a Plan

We may never fully understand what God's plan is for our children. Nor can we hasten the plan in any way, since it must unfold in God's own time. Our job as parents is to encourage, pray, and communicate to our children the fact that they are important enough for God to lead them by His indwelling Spirit. This constant and consistent feedback will help them see the importance of God's plan and help them be open to His leading, day by day.

> *11 For I know the plans I have for you, says the Lord. They are plans for good and not for evil, to give you a future and a hope.*
> *12 In those days when you pray, I will listen.*
> *13 You will find me when you seek me, if you look for me in earnest.*
> —Jeremiah 29:11-13 (TLB)

The Book of 2 Peter gives us more insight into how God works out His plans in our lives:

> *3 His divine power has given us everything we need for life and godliness through our knowledge of him who called us by his own glory and goodness.*
> *4 Through these he has given us his very great and precious promises, so that through them you may participate in the*

divine nature and escape the corruption in the world
caused by evil desires. . . .
10 Therefore, my brothers, be all the more eager to make
your calling and election sure. For if you do these things,
you will never fall,
11 and you will receive a rich welcome into the eternal
kingdom of our Lord and Savior Jesus Christ.
—2 Peter 1:3-4, 10-11 (NIV)

Peter is making it clear that there is a special place in God's grand scheme of things—even for us. He assures us that it's through this plan that we and our children can escape corruption and the evil desires of the world.

Our children are faced with situations today that we never even dreamed about as kids. The excessive violence, drug use, and premarital sexual activity serve to corrupt our society and threaten our children's faith. Peter assures us that God has a plan and that we and our children are part of it. He then reminds us that the power to overcome does not reside within us, but proceeds from God alone.

Verse 10 speaks of a calling. This word in the Greek refers to an invitation and has the idea of "blessings" associated with it. Our children are important because they are part of God's plan; and He has a special invitation for them to join and be active participants in it. We must trust enough to help our children follow God's plan for them. As they experience God's leading within them, they'll begin to sense how special they are.

YOU'RE SO SPECIAL!

Remember being on the playground when it was time to choose teams? How about those pick-up games of basketball or softball? The two "captains" (chosen by popular acclaim) would start filling their rosters, alternately calling out one kid's name at a time. God forbid that you'd be the last person chosen. What an ignominious distinction—being the kid neither team wanted! You certainly weren't cool if you landed at the bottom of the athletic talent list, but it was worse, of course, if you weren't chosen at all.

No one feels special when left off the team. No one feels special when pushed aside or compared unfavorably with the talented few. Yet it's true that some kids are better players than others. Just as some adults are smarter than you and more successful, richer, or more holy. Are we still "special"? Are our children special, too, even the ones riding the pines on the sidelines?

Your Child Is a Gift from God

> *3 Behold, children are a gift of the LORD; The fruit of the womb is a reward.*
> *4 Like arrows in the hand of a warrior, So are the children of one's youth.*
> *5 How blessed is the man whose quiver is full of them; They shall not be ashamed, When they speak with their enemies in the gate.*
> —Psalm 127:3-5 (NASB)

Yes, regardless of talent or ability, we're all special in God's eyes. It's up to us parents to realize that our children are special gifts from the Lord and then communicate that passionately to them. They were not an accident, God created them, and they should be welcome members of our home. They have value and they have worth. Why? Because they are gifts and they are a reward. Too often children are seen as liabilities instead of recognized for the value they add to the family. How could something valued so highly by God be a mere "inconvenience"?

Hannah is an excellent example of how to manage these precious gifts from God. "In bitterness of soul Hannah wept much and prayed to the Lord" (1 Sam. 1:10). Hannah was a childless woman in a society that viewed bearing sons as the ultimate fulfillment for a woman. Her pain was the same felt by every person who says, "I'm a useless failure." In Hannah's case, the wound was kept open by the constant provocation of her husband's second wife, Peninnah, who had several children and took perverse pleasure in tormenting Hannah over her barrenness.

For years, Hannah wept before the Lord when the family attended the religious festivals held regularly at Shiloh, where the tabernacle stood during much of the Judges era. Finally Hannah made a vow, a promise that if God gave her a son she would give him for service to God at the tabernacle. What marvelous lessons to learn from this brief chapter!

Larry Richards writes:

The biographies of many Christian leaders tell of mothers who, even before they became pregnant, gave their future children to the Lord. Many years after I was led to go into the ministry, my own mother told how she had made a similar dedication—and followed it up with a lifetime of prayers that my sister and I might both serve God. We owe so much to godly mothers who see their children as gifts from God intended to be given back to Him.[4]

Hannah most certainly looked upon her son as a gift from a loving God. After years of waiting, she must have had a heart filled with joy when she gave birth. Then she lived up to her commitment and gave her son as a gift back to the One who had provided.

Seeing our children as gifts may not be easy at times! But remember: Jesus sees people differently than we do; perhaps Scripture can help us broaden our perspective. . . .

• *See what's inside them.* We tend to look at the external appearances while God looks at the heart. First Samuel 16:7b says "Do not look at his appearance or at the height of his stature, because I have rejected him; for God sees not as man sees, for man looks at the outward appearance, but the LORD looks at the heart" (NASB). The scene depicts Samuel looking for a new king. The Lord tells him to visit Jesse and that Samuel will find the new king there. The first of Jesse's sons was Eliab, and by all appearances he should be king; he was so tall and muscular. Isn't that what a king should look like? But God looks at the heart.

Every child is entitled to hold up his or her head, not in haughtiness, but in confidence and security. This is the concept of human worth intended by our Creator. How foolish for us to doubt our value when He formed us in His own image! His view of the beauty cult was made abundantly clear more than three thousand years ago when

Samuel was seeking a King of Israel. Samuel naturally selected the tallest, handsomest son of Jesse, but God told him he had chosen the wrong man. . . . Despite the clarity of this message, we have not taught it to our children. Some little folk feel so inferior, they can't believe even God could love them. They feel so totally worthless and empty, thinking that God neither cares nor understands.[5]

I have seen so many parents focus on externals instead of "internals" with their children. They look, not deep into the soul of this child, but at what the child can or can't do or (supposedly) become. In our shortsightedness we focus on such tangible things. God has given us a precious gift, and He is the ultimate interior decorator. He alone knows the heart of this gift, this child of ours, and yet we insist on judging what we can't see.

•*See what they're becoming, day by day.* We tend to look only at what they are right now. The Bible says, "if any [person] is in Christ, he is a new creature; the old things passed away; behold, new things have come" (2 Cor. 5:17, NASB). Instead of envisioning what our children can become, we often make the mistake of obsessing over what they are today. Children need time to develop and parents need to understand fully what their child is today and what she could become tomorrow. Paul says we can, with Christ, become new creations. God looks at our children with a different set of eyes and expectations than we parents often do.

How limiting that can be for us! Would it be fair if God looked at us at our conversion and said, "Well, that's about as good as Jane can become," or "That's just the way it's going to be with Joe"? I hardly think any of us would make the grade as Christians if we didn't have that new-creature promise from Paul.

Bible teacher Warren Wiersbe points out that "our new relationship to Christ has brought about a new relationship to the world and the people around us. We no longer look at life the way we used to."[6] Because "all things are become new," we also have a new view of people around us. We see them as sinners for whom Christ died. We no longer see them as kids, friends, or enemies. We can see them as Christ sees them *and as He appreciates them.*

Ann Douglas, in an Internet article titled "How to Make Your

Child Feel Special" provides some practical tips on the subject:

Help Your Child Recognize what Makes Her Unique
Parents should make a point of acknowledging such traits as honesty, courage, insight, and creativity, heaping on praise where praise is due. It takes twenty seconds to make someone's day.

Be Generous in Your Praise
Be sure that it's sincere and specific. Children are more likely to accept praise that sounds heartfelt rather than contrived.

Talk to Your Children about Things that Really Matter to Them
Parents can help their children feel valued if they take time to listen to what their children are really trying to communicate.

Understand Your Child's Unique Temperament
Accept each person for what he or she is—just as you expect others to accept and love you the way you are.

Celebrate Regularly
Celebrate all the little things that deserve to be savored on a day-to-day basis.

You Are There for Them
Believe in your child when he is the shakiest. Remember that Winston Churchill had to repeat the sixth grade!

Laugh with Your Child
There is nothing like shared laughter to foster a bond between parent and child. Sharing inside jokes reminds your child that he or she has a very special place in your heart.

Share Something of Yourself
Tell them about the times that you failed to hit the mark in life. Be the first to admit that you have made a mistake, particularly if that mistake affects your children. Ask for their forgiveness.[7]

Your Child Can Develop Positive Self-Esteem

As children accept their specialness in God and in their families, they naturally develop positive self-esteem. Dr. Kevin Leman, in his book *Becoming the Parent God Wants You to Be*, lays out a simple, yet powerful foundation for building self-esteem in your children. His suggestions require a huge investment of energy, but it will pay huge dividends. It will also take time—a lifetime.

"A" is for Acceptance and Affirmation. "Children who feel

accepted and affirmed tell themselves, 'Hey, Mom and Dad love me, no matter what. They really care about me.' Acceptance means being loved unconditionally for who you are, not how you perform or what you do. Affirmation helps a child know he or she is valued as a unique individual, not in comparison to someone else."[8]

"B" is for Belonging. Robert Frost may have said it best, "Home is the place where, when you have to go there, they have to take you in." It sounds harsh, but it's true—nowhere but home feels like home, and these are the folks who take you in.[9] Nothing has illustrated this point more to Pam and me than when we moved our family to Michigan. We left California in December of 1989 when Jennifer was right in the middle of her junior year in high school. A terrible time to move, but we had no choice. By the time Jennifer transferred into her new school, she found that friendships were already made, groups were well formed. She admits that without our family to come home to each day, without a sense from Pam and me of real belonging, she would have made some bad choices and lost her feeling of self-esteem. We helped her experience at least one place—our home—as safe, warm, and encouraging. She could be rejected at school and not like it at all. But she could also feel the security of belonging, with unconditional acceptance, to our family.

"C" is for Competence. "Children with a good self-image feel capable. They face a challenge and tell themselves, "I can do it!"[10] This is not the same as feeling that one's self-worth is based only on performance. Rather, a sense of competence has more to do with one's identity as a capable, worthy person, one who fulfills responsibilities and lives with accountability. Parents can help instill this identity as they encourage, support, and say, "Go for it! You can do it!"

Many times Pam and I watched our children launching out to try something new and exciting. I don't want to embarrass them, but they did try some things that didn't play to their strengths; sometimes they weren't highly successful. As their parents, however, we didn't view these endeavors as bad for them. We let them try, and we cheered them on in spite of the results. It would have been so wrong for us to criticize. And after all, don't all of us look back at certain crazy mistakes and serious misjudgments, only to see them now as priceless learning experiences?

AROUND HERE, IT'S OK TO FAIL

Your kids deserve an environment that encourages them to succeed. They also need, if you are to TRUST enough to love, an environment that allows them to fail. I know this may run counter to your approach so far, but do you realize that nothing great has ever been achieved without a degree of failure first? Suppose Edison had given up after his first few hundred experimental failures with potential light bulb filaments? Suppose Honest Abe Lincoln had stopped running for office after his numerous defeats? Suppose Jesus had stopped preaching in the face of heckling crowds and slanderous rejections? Think of the countless inventions, ideas, and discoveries that could only have happened with the help of repeated failures.

Failure—Necessary for Growth

Yes, our children need to feel love and acceptance in spite of their failures. After all, God loves us, not because of our goodness but because of our failure. He loves us *because* we are sinners.

A few books have really changed my life, and one of them was published in 1982 by two consultants named Tom Peters and Robert Waterman, Jr. Their book *In Search of Excellence* put me on a path to not only be a better leader, but a better father as well. The book delivered some startling truths about teamwork, and it offered interesting insights into failure.

> *A special attribute of the success-oriented, positive, and innovating environment is a substantial tolerance for failure. James Burke, Johnson & Johnson's CEO, says one of [their company's] tenets is that "you've got to be willing to fail." He adds that General Johnson, J & J's founder, said to him, "If I wasn't making mistakes, I wasn't making decisions."* . . . *Champions have to make lots of tries and consequently suffer some failures or the organization won't learn.*[11]

I can restate Peters and Waterman (with all due respect) and say that *children have to make lots of tries and consequently suffer some failures or they won't learn.* The greatest hazard in life is to risk nothing. Your children won't learn, grow, feel, change, love, or live without risking and sometimes failing. Children need to be motivated and stretched in their lives, and failure can certainly motivate them toward growth. Children may feel uncomfortable as they stretch and learn (or try new things). But, of course, God promises no one a comfortable existence; He does promise His presence in all circumstances. Therefore, parents need to be supportive and encouraging and applaud every try—whether it's a winner or not. Simply stated, that means giving your children every chance for success.

> *John Wooden, one of the most successful basketball coaches of all time, focused upon the growing process. In* Six Timeless Marketing Blunders, *William Shanklin writes about Wooden's approach to coaching. Shanklin tells that while Wooden coached UCLA, he didn't stress winning. He emphasized preparation, teamwork, a willingness to change, and the desire for each person to perform at peak potential. His focus was on the process, not the end product.[12]*

Sometimes the focus of parents is too much on "winning" and not enough on the process. I've always been intrigued watching parents as their child is learning to walk. They carefully hold the little tyke up; he balances for a moment, and then . . . *wham!* He hits the floor. Baby gets up, balances, and *wham!* He hits the floor. This process goes on and on. The parents have such patience, the baby keeps on trying. Then one day it finally happens. Little Freddy or little Joyce takes a solo step. Wow! You'd think the greatest thing in the world had just happened. (And at that moment, for those parents, it has!)

In a few more days, the little child takes some more steps. Daddy or Mommy position themselves on the floor. They extend their arms, and the cute little child walks two or three steps. The child teeters, she wobbles, but she makes it to the elated parent. They call the grandparents; everyone at the office is treated to pictures. What an amazing piece of parental support!

Now fast-forward ten years. This same child is struggling to make a short speech at school, or he's having problems understanding fractions. Do Mom and Dad put the same skills to work?

Hardly. They criticize, "How could you be shy?" Or they compare, "When your sister had fractions, she got straight A's!" Why is helping, coaching, and celebrating when baby takes a stumbling step so different from helping, coaching, and celebrating when Johnny gets a B on his test? Where do we go wrong?

Failure—Expectations Too High?

Children are children. So do we set our expectations for them too high? Can it be a matter of taking *ourselves* too seriously?

I have never met Mike Singletary, but I deeply admire him. In a sense, I do feel I know him because of his twelve years as an All-Pro linebacker with the Chicago Bears. He earned the NFL's "Defensive Player of the Year" award three times and was named the "1990 NFL Man of the Year." I've observed Mike through all of this.

During the games, it seemed the television camera would always catch Mike as he was staring across the line of scrimmage at the opposition. His eyes would bulge wide open, his complete concentration undeniable, and it was obvious that he was in total control of his defense. Mike was intimidating, quick, a brutally hard hitter on the field. You'd think he would set the highest expectations for everyone else too. He writes:

> *It would be a tragedy if my kids grew up knowing only that their dad was a good football player and husband and father. If I expected them to live every minute of their lives the way they have seen me live as they grew up, they would be frustrated and devastated if they ever failed. I want them to know what they didn't see, when I failed miserably and only came out of it by the grace of God. . . . I also want them to know of my mistakes because they will make their own, and I don't want them to feel they are the first person in the family to fail. . . . Most of all, I want them to know that by the grace of God, he brought me through it and out of it, and he can do the same for them.*[13]

Expectations can definitely influence a child's behavior. And setting the bar too high may be something that discourages rather than encourages. In a live presentation years ago, Tom Peters said, "You can put a man in eight feet of water and expect some success, but put him in twelve feet of water without hope, and he will drown." Children, therefore, must have expectations that are rooted in reality and not rooted in something unattainable, damaging, or outside their areas of strength.

It would be ridiculous for me to expect Jennifer to excel in math. She just never grasped the intricacies of certain mathematical principles. I worked with her, and she received tutoring from teachers, but she didn't do well. It was something low on her list of talents and gifts. But put her in front of people as a performer, and she will exceed all expectations. She once entered a speaking contest in high school. She did so well that she received coverage from our hometown newspaper. Her subject was abortion, and she was passionate about it. She took a very conservative approach and our local newspaper, in spite of its liberal reputation, ate it up. Jennifer exceeded any expectations we might have had because we weren't asking her for anything except her reward for a job well done. She was acting in her area of giftedness, and it was easy for her to excel.

I so appreciate professional golfers and their mental approach to the game. Most don't necessarily compete against each other; they compete against the course and themselves. They set expectations of themselves not based on peer pressure, but on their own expectations. So these golfers can feel good about their performance while still losing a tournament. That is a foreign concept to many, but I think it's a healthy one.

Failure—Essential for Learning

How else could we learn life's most valuable lessons, if we don't risk, try, and sometimes fail? Yet we often forget the powerful lessons a little failure can bring into our children's lives.

I've already alluded to Zachary's final year of high school. He was facing the possibility of not being accepted into the college he'd handpicked. He had no second choice but had brought on a situation that could hurt him academically. Pam and I made a choice to allow him to learn from his mistakes. We probably could have come to his rescue, but the mistake became a lifelong lesson for him, and our intervention would have gotten in the way of that learning. Our involvement would have blocked the lesson God wanted to teach him.

Do not think this works only with older children. Returning to the example of a toddler learning to walk, how successful would that toddler be if we never let him fall down? On the other hand, when a young child begins to learn how to rollerblade or ride a bicycle, how valuable is that simple process of falling down? The only way we can learn balance is by making adjustments to our mistakes.

King David made some mistakes in his life, as well. The man after God's own heart, the psalmist, the leader, the great king failed miserably. As I have said earlier, many great leaders have failed, and all of history records David's failures. That doesn't mean we do not fail. We just don't have our dirty laundry hanging out as David does! In 1 Chronicles 21, David has one of his less famous adventures in failure. Here David is convinced that he needs to take a census. Pride gets hold of the king and he wants to count, against God's advice, how many soldiers are in Israel.

What is interesting about this Scripture passage is that the same eight circumstances that helped David learn from his failure with Bathsheba are present in this event as well. Consider:

- God sends someone to confront his sin (v. 3)
- David admits he has done wrong (v. 8)
- He takes responsibility (v. 17)
- He trusts God's mercy (v. 13)
- He demonstrates sincerity (vv. 18-19)
- He renewed fellowship with God (v. 22)
- He changed his attitude (v. 24)
- David looked to the future (v. 22)

David's pattern of failure—and learning from failure—is a wonderful example for us as we raise our children. We can all learn from failure, but we as parents have a wonderful opportunity to help our children develop positive habits on how they can handle failure and continuing trusting God in all things.

If we encourage our children as they experience personal failures (no matter how big or small) we will see (and more importantly, they will see) some great things rise out of those failures. As I write this, Zachary is a student at his dream college. Like David, he learned from his failures, repented, changed his attitude, kept his eyes forward . . . and God did the rest.[14]

This can happen with your children as well. As long as you TRUST enough to love them. Help them to know how important they really are—they are fearfully and wonderfully made. Help them to understand they are special to you and to God. Lastly, help them learn from their failures. TRUST God enough to give them the love they need, the encouragement to move forward, and the attitude to realize that God remains in loving control.

THINK AND TALK ABOUT IT

1. What is something about each of your children's personalities that is unique?
2. How will you help your children add a godly quality to their faith today?
3. In what way do you need to encourage each of your children this week?
4. How could you show your children that they are important?

Notes

1 Patrick M. Morley, *The Rest of Your Life: Your Personal Plan for Finding Authentic Meaning and Significance* (Nashville: Thomas Nelson Publishers, Inc., 1992), 181-182.

2 Beverly Levitt, "Burning Onions with Leah Adler," *The Tribune*, September 26, 1999.

3 Beverly LaHaye, *How to Develop Your Child's Temperament* (Medford, OR: Harvest House Publishers, 1974), 52.

4 Lawrence O. Richards, *365-Day Devotional Commentary*, Ed. 2, QuickVerse 5.0

5 James Dobson, *The New Hide or Seek: Building Self-Esteem in Your Child* (Grand Rapids, MI: Fleming H. Revell), 72.

6 Warren Wiersbe, *The Bible Exposition Commentary, New Testament* (Colorado Springs: Chariot Victor Publishing).

7 Ann Douglas, "How to Make Your Child Feel Special," © FAMILY.COM, 1999.

8 Kevin Leman, *Becoming the Parent God Wants You to Be* (Colorado Springs:

NavPress, 1998), 108.

9 Robert Frost, "Death of a Hired Hand," *Leadership Journal*, Vol. 10, No. 1.

10 Kevin Leman, *Becoming the Parent God Wants You to Be*, 110.

11 Thomas J. Peters and Robert H. Waterman, Jr., *In Search of Excellence: Lessons from America's Best-Run Companies* (New York: Harper and Row, 1982), 223.

12 John C. Maxwell, *Developing the Leaders Around You: How to Help Others Reach Their Full Potential* (Nashville: Thomas Nelson Publishers, 1995), 120.

13 Mike Singletary, in *Men's Devotional Bible* (Grand Rapids, MI: Zondervan Publishing House, 1993), 475.

14 Portions of this Bible study on David came from notes from the sermon, "Can Christ Use My Failures?" presented by John Maxwell, at Skyline Wesleyan Church, Lemon Grove, CA, August 12, 1984.

Chapter 6

TRUSTING ENOUGH TO LISTEN

I CAN STILL SEE THOSE PRETTY GRAY EYES smiling back at me. They belonged to Miss Hempstead, the best high school English teacher a kid could have. Why such accolades? For one thing, I knew that when I walked up to talk to Miss Hempstead there'd be nothing more important to her than *this precious moment* when I had something to say. And she always looked me straight in the eye.

You see, as we conversed, the whole world revolved around me—yes, me!—though time came to a complete standstill. For as long as I wanted to be King of the Earth.

That fine teacher really knew how to listen to kids. Do you know how to do it? Listening to your children is the greatest gift you can bring to the parent-child relationship. When they come to you with a problem, an idea, or just to talk, they need to feel that they are in control of that time. Listening provides key sources of information about our children. It we aren't listening, that information source dries up. Uncertainty arises, a feeling of disconnection, and a sad superficiality begins to pervade the environment.

We live in an area close to the beach, and we often need to drive in the fog. We know the streets and highways well; however, in the fog, it all falls apart. We feel disoriented, fear we'll hit something, and even on familiar turf, we can't "see" where we are going or measure how far we've gone. The same is true for children as they attempt to communicate to a non-listening parent. They're fogged in, frustrated that they are doing the best they can but getting nowhere.

Jesus said: "Anyone who is willing to hear should listen and understand!" (Matt. 11:15, NLT). He was giving testimony to John the Baptist and ended by telling the people to "listen up!" Being *willing* to hear means setting aside any preconceived ideas or prejudices before attending to the speaker. If we aren't willing to hear, then everything someone says to us will go right past our ears. Yet God gave us two ears and one mouth; too bad we use our mouth twice as much as our ears! How many times have you been telling a story, and you know that the person supposedly listening is forming her own comeback as you speak? Such people aren't "willing to hear." They're interested, but only in what *they* have to say.

In our home, when our children were allowed simply to talk without interruption, they often worked out their problems themselves. More often than not, when we just listened, they thought through what they'd done (in the case of poor behavior) or thought through the problem, and came up with excellent plans and solutions. From there, our job was to affirm and encourage as they took action.

It all comes down to being "willing to hear" when our children speak. We look them in the eye, make our time stand still, and place them on the throne. At that moment, we free ourselves of distractions and completely focus our attention. Yes, no matter how trivial the concern, we focus. Then when the weightier issues arise, the children keep coming to us. But this kind of listening takes some doing; it's certainly not a passive endeavor.

READY FOR ACTIVE LISTENING?

I've spent most of my professional career in front of customers. To be successful in this, I had to learn how to listen—it was best for the customer, and it was best for the profitability and service reputation of my company. The customers were happy, and the company was happy because it was able to learn and adapt to changing customer needs. All around, it was a win-win situation.

Sadly, most people think that in order to persuade they need to be good at talking. A typical "real good talker" believes he or she can *tell* the customer (or, in a family, the children) and they will automatically "buy it." When it comes to business success, though, I'd rather have on my team the interested introvert over the interesting extrovert. A good businessperson (or parent) is like a great detective.

She listens intently to her "customer" and takes the time to read every signal that comes through in words, body language, and attitude.

On the other hand, if you take control of the conversation, you'll usually oversell or miss the objective completely. I can remember coming to conversations with my children (or a customer, for that matter) fully prepared to deliver the solution. When the meeting finished, however, my child was unhappy because I had my mind made up before gathering all the pertinent information. Sort of like saying, "Don't confuse me with the facts, Ma'am." But then we're faced with repairing a relationship—damage that could have been avoided if we'd just listened in the first place.

So let's get very practical about how to listen actively. The next two sections of this chapter will focus on two important approaches (and their related skills) that have helped Pam and me develop listening ears. The first involves learning the habit of *asking questions*, the other is *seeking to understand* before trying to be understood.

Questioning Your Way to Understanding

My wife has the wonderful ability to dig for truth and find the reasons behind a behavior or attitude. She's successful, for the most part, because of her ability to ask questions. In a sense, Pam is a master sleuth. She probes and explores, uncovering what's underneath all the surface information immediately at hand. She listens and asks questions, poses the same question in different ways, then raises it at different times. Her ability to inquire with gentle goodwill has helped us both listen better to our children.

The call to question, to dig deeper, can easily cause FEAR to rear its ugly head. Many parents would rather flee this type of encounter with their children. For the short-term, it's easier just to ignore the children instead of mining for what else may be behind their words and deeds. TRUSTing enough to listen and ask questions means that we boldly seek God's help in using questions to keep the conversation alive.

Asking questions is a vital sign of healthy parental curiosity. Questions show our children that we are interested in what they're saying and we want to learn from them. Asking questions in this context shows we are open, excited, and have a willingness to get involved at a deeper level. "Children can tell whether they have a parent's interest and attention by the way the parent replies or does not reply."[1]

Parents certainly do not want to put themselves in the position of the disciples when they heard things from Jesus but were afraid to ask any clarifying questions.

31b He was teaching his disciples. He said to them, "The Son of Man is going to be betrayed into the hands of men. They will kill him, and after three days he will rise."
32 But they did not understand what he meant and were afraid to ask him about it.
—Mark 9:31-32 (NIV)

No doubt this was an intense lesson from Jesus to the disciples. But how much clearer would they have understood if they had asked some simple questions?

Repeatedly he had told them what awaited him in Jerusalem, and yet they were still thinking of his Kingdom in earthly terms and of themselves as his chief ministers of state. There is something heartbreaking in the thought of Jesus going towards a cross and his disciples arguing about who would be greatest.[2]

The disciples remind us of ourselves. We go into a situation and think we know all the answers, have the future all figured out. Then someone, in this case Jesus, wants to communicate with us and we do not listen. The disciples didn't understand because they chose not to listen and they chose not to ask good questions.

What's the solution? Over the years, I've categorized questioning techniques that have helped me keep the conversation rolling.

• ***Tying Down the Details.*** This type of question helps you tie down the details and gives you a good idea if you fully understand what your child is saying. For example, you may say, "You want to go outside and play for an hour, isn't that right?" You not only restate something the child has said, you ask a question for clarification of details. When you get agreement you can be fairly certain that you are on the same page. If you receive a blank stare or a confident "That's not what I said," then you know you have some more talking to do. Some of the most effective tie-downs are:

Isn't it?	Doesn't it?	Hasn't he?	Haven't they?
Don't you?	Didn't you?	Shouldn't we?	Couldn't we?
Isn't that right?	Won't you?	Is that it?	Do I have it right?

The goal is to find out whether what you heard is actually what they said. You're showing them you understand. You can then follow up a tie-down question with another question, but at the very least you are showing your child that you are listening and that both of you are agreeing on what has been said or promised.

• *Alternate Choice.* This technique allows you to ask a question that offers at least two choices. Here the child begins to use discernment and your conversation becomes much more of a dialog. The technique, like the previous one, also helps the parent get some details. For example, "You want to play soccer with Jimmy, don't you? Will you want to go Saturday or Friday after school?" Remember the goal is to enlist your child in conversation, letting her know you are actively listening.

Alternate choice also lets you set some parameters if, for example, you know that only a few solutions will solve a problem. You may not want to dictate a solution, so the alternate choice question allows you to present the acceptable solutions in the form of a "choice" question. It allows you to guide the child with "which do you think" type questions that serve to bring him or her into the problem solving.

Using an alternate choice question also lets you avoid asking an open-ended question that might broaden the discussion too wide for the reality of the moment. "Where do you want to go for dinner?" opens the discussion much more widely than, "Would Mexican or Chinese be better tonight?"

Alternate choice questions can also help you offer guidance without resorting to demands or arguments. Let's say your son doesn't like to read, but he needs to read a book for school. Rather than attacking his lack of interest, find two great books and bring them home saying, "Which of these do you think you'd like to read?"

• *Easily Answered Questions.* These are great discussion facilitators. The technique involves using the time-honored Socratic method. Parents can ask some simple, loving questions that will guide the child's thinking so that he or she discovers new truths and insights. You want to help them explore and analyze, because if children fail to sort through all that they are hearing, feeling, and seeing they may make some wrong choices.

Should you find it difficult to ask these questions, why not start with the five "W" and "H" questions used in writing news reports? Ask: "Who?" "What?" "When?" "Where?" "Why?" and "How?"

• *"If" Questions.* Sometimes it isn't easy to talk to our children. They may require an environment where there is very little risk before opening up. "If" questions take your children out of reality and ask them to use their imagination to answer a hypothetical question. "If we were going to let you go to the concert, how would you get there?" is an example that gets the conversation going before you've committed to anything. You're testing the waters, probing for their best guess, not pressuring for the right answer, right at this moment. "If" questions also give you a solid idea as to what your children are thinking. Simply start with "if" and then lead into the possible answer. "If you were allowed to go . . . when would you . . . how would you . . . where would you . . . what kind would you . . . and so on.

• *Silent Sam.* What about the child who just doesn't seem to want to open up? How can parents get him to talk and communicate? Norm Wright and Rex Johnson, in their book *Communication: Key to Your Teens*, write the following about a character they call Silent Sam:

> *Many have said, "I'd love to communicate, but how can you with a brick wall!" If your teenager fits this description, ask yourself the question, what is his silence saying? What is the message behind the silence? It could communicate love, satisfaction, well-being, pouting, sulking, indifference, hostility, bitterness or fear.*

What can you do to help the silent member open up? Saying "talk to me" usually doesn't help. Ask for opinions and avoid questions that can be responded to with a "yep" or "nope." Ask, "What do you think about. . .?" or "What would you suggest . . .?" If he says, "I don't know," you could offer three or four suggestions.

Don't put pressure on your teenager. You might say, "I am willing to talk with you so when you feel you would like to talk, let me know." Then back off, pray for an abundance of patience, and wait.[3]

Understanding Before Being Understood

Stephen R. Covey, in his book *The 7 Habits of Highly Effective People,* encourages people to seek first to understand, then to be understood. This is a powerful principle for parents to employ with their children. People, for the most part, generally do not listen in order to be informed; they listen in order to reply. In one "Family Circus" cartoon, the little girl is looking up at her father as he reads the newspaper. She says to him, "Daddy, you have to listen to me with your eyes as well as your ears." She was frustrated, but how much more upset would our children be if we were looking at them while they spoke and still our answer had nothing to do with what they'd been saying?

John Gray, in his book *Men Are from Mars, Women Are from Venus,* illustrates how men are always trying to solve problems, while women just want to vent or have someone listen to them. Unfortunately, I think parent and child communication can fall into the same rut. Parents quickly offer a dictator-like solution—and there may not even be a problem! The children may just want to talk, perhaps venting some frustrations of the day; instead, they get another lecture.

Parents need to be patient and understand what their children are saying before they attempt to be understood. Covey writes:

A father once told me, "I can't understand my kid. He just won't listen to me at all."

"Let me restate what you just said," I replied. "You don't understand your son because he won't listen to you?"

"That's right," he replied.

"Let me try this again," I said. "You don't understand your son because he won't listen to you?"

"That's what I said," he impatiently replied.

"I thought that to understand another person, you needed to listen to him," I suggested.

"Oh!" he said. There was a long pause. "Oh!" he said again, as the light began to dawn. "Oh, yeah! But I do understand him. I know what he is going through. I went through the same thing myself. I guess what I don't understand is why he won't listen to me."

This man didn't have the vaguest idea of what was really going on inside the boy's head. He looked into his own head, and thought he saw the world, including his boy.[4]

Nowhere in my search of the Scriptures can I see any importance placed upon our opinions being understood. What I find is that we struggle to have God listen to us, and God struggles to have us "understand" His message for us. The psalm writers continually ask God to listen but they don't, to my knowledge, seek to have God understand their point of view (circumstances, problems, and concerns, yes; however, not their opinion). We cry out to God and hope to receive His instructions *because He already fully understands our needs.*

God communicates to us throughout the Bible, and in every case, He is asking that we take the time to understand His message. He gives His people, the Jews, hall-of-fame leaders—judges, kings, and prophets. He finally sends His message straight from heaven in the form of His Son, to disclose all things related to salvation and the purpose of history. Yet we do not seek to understand God, in many cases, any more than we seek to understand our children.

Many of the Psalms provide a model of seeking first to understand. We read in Psalm 5:

2 Listen to my cry for help, my King and my God, for I will never pray to anyone but you.

3 Listen to my voice in the morning, LORD. Each morning

I bring my requests to you and wait expectantly.
—Psalm 5:2-3 (NLT)

Here the psalmist is crying out to the Lord to listen. Literally, he's saying, "Pay close attention" to my cry for help. When children come to us for help, they are asking us to be attentive to what they have to say. They need their parents, and they expect their parents will actively listen.

In verse 3, the psalmist asks again for God to listen. This time he uses another word. This Hebrew word means "to hear," and it carries with it a connotation of understanding. So: "Pay close attention and understand me." This is the same cry coming from our children. They come to their parents for understanding and hope that their parents will "hear" with their ears, eyes, and hearts. Covey writes,

Empathetic listening is so powerful because it gives you accurate data to work with. Instead of projecting your own autobiography and assuming thoughts, feelings, motives and interpretation, you are dealing with the reality inside another person's head and heart. You're listening to understand. You're focused on receiving the deep communication of another human soul.[5]

Proverbs says, "Any story sounds true until someone tells the other side and sets the record straight" (Prov. 18:17, TLB). When we do not seek first to understand, we hear only one side of the story. Many times, it is our side of the story through our grid of experience, our grid of understanding, and our grid of prejudice. The proverb asks us to consider both sides, which means actively listening to the speaker. There are some obvious ways we can tell if we are actively listening, as shown in the chart on page 114.

One thing to remember: there is a difference between understanding and acceptance. Understanding does not mean approval. It simply means you comprehend what the speaker is trying to communicate. You are trying to "walk in their shoes" for a while before you speak.

TRUSTing enough to listen means asking questions of your children, trying hard to understand what they have to say before you

Passive Listener	Active Listener
• Listens with answer already formed in his head. • Completes the statement or question for the speaker. • Interrupts the speaker. • Interrupts the speaker with nonverbal messages. • Judges what is being said.	• Waits for speaker to completely talk and asks questions to clarify, get more details, or to make certain she totally understands what the speaker has said. • Patiently absorbs what is being said. Resists the temptation to rush the speaker. • Waits until a natural break in the conversation and only interrupts to ask clarifying questions. • Makes sure not to nervously rearrange papers, sit in a downgrading position, look around the room, and shift focus to something or someone else. Stops what he is doing and completely focuses on the speaker. • Understands what is being said in spite of the tone of voice or topic, before sharing an opinion.

give your answer or opinion. It also means learning some new skills—listening skills.

PRACTICE SKILLFUL LISTENING!

Listening isn't a school subject. You won't see it on any college curriculum. Many people believe it is a natural skill (after all, we have two ears) and that as long as we hear the "critical" things in our lives, we are all right. It is estimated that 50 to 75 percent of our time is spent listening, yet comprehension tests reveal that we aren't remembering what we hear.

Prepare Yourself for Listening

Good listening requires patience and practice. Ask any parent who has tried listening to her teenager as he asks permission to step across well-known boundaries. Occasionally, when we are in the heat of debate, we may forget the simple steps to good listening. Therefore, I've included all the steps, just in case you may need a refresher course.

• *Create an atmosphere for listening.* When your children come home from school, stop what you're doing and listen. When you greet them after a long day, set aside a few minutes just to focus on what they want to talk about. Make yourself available to them, do not simply nod your head and continue what you're doing. Shut off the TV or radio when you sense they want to talk. Decide, up front, not to answer the telephone if it rings.

Pam and I set aside two special times for parent-child conversations. One opportunity came during our nightly devotionals. We studied the Bible or simple Bible stories with our children and the questions at the end of the stories got us all to talking. It was a great time of "no-pressure" sharing with our children. We learned lots about their needs, their dreams, and their goals. We were also able to help them shape their values in a nonthreatening environment.

The second special time for conversation occurred while we were in the car together. For example, we had good conversations as one of us took the kids to school. We were not looking down at them, but we were equals in those car seats. We could talk and laugh, and no one on the outside could hear what we said. Riding in the car became a good time of learning and appreciating each other.

• Listen patiently. Most people think faster than they speak, so it's often easy for parents to think ahead of their children. Small children with limited vocabularies aren't sure of themselves as they present what's on their minds. Nevertheless, listen as though their ideas are the only thing on your mind. Focus your complete attention upon that little one. Decide, in the beginning, to be a patient listener.

Avoid cutting children off in mid-sentence or before they have finished. If we aren't ready to understand before being understood, we risk ending the conversation before it begins. One tactic that worked for us was to postpone a discussion if we really didn't have time that moment. We would explain to the kids that we were busy, let them know why we couldn't talk at the moment, and then agree on when we could give them our undivided attention. They could see we were setting priorities—and they *are* a priority, just not right now.

• Be ready to read nonverbal messages. Many messages flow to us from childrens' tone of voice, body language, facial expressions, level of energy, and posture. Be ready to read these messages like a book! You can learn as much from these subtle messages as you would from the actual words being spoken.

Prepare Your Children for Talking

Some children need an invitation to talk to us. You may need to begin with "tell me about your day." They may feel more comfortable and more appreciated if their parents asked them about themselves, what they did, and how they responded to certain events.

Continuing to ask questions will help you pry out the details and enjoy an engaging conversation. Here are some other things you can do:

• Demonstrate your interest. Get excited when they come to you and want to talk. Reinforce their positive behavior with positive behavior of your own—show that you are very interested in what they are saying. Lead them to a chair; pull up a chair of your own. Be a Miss Hempstead and drill your eyes into theirs. "You, my child, are so intriguing!"

• Extend the conversation. This is somewhat related to asking questions. Parents should pick up pieces of the conversation and ask questions about it. The goal is to have the child elaborate on things. Restate what she's saying. Play it back for her and get agreement. If, for some reason, you don't get agreement, then you know you haven't successfully understood. Remember that you can't respond appropriately before you completely understand.

• Use their own words to reflect feelings. Many times you can extend conversations by simply saying, "You sound uptight; what's up?" In this case, the parent is reflecting the feelings he's observed. This is a powerful tool for helping children talk. It involves watching and knowing your children so when you see them in a quandary or angry, or simply down, you can ask them a reflective question and then let them respond.

Reflecting feelings is a great way to communicate, keeping us from jumping in with an answer before the appropriate time. We just repeat what they're saying and leave open space for their elaboration:

Teen: "I had a rotten day at school."
Parent: "Oh, so you're feeling hassled today?"

Teen: "I can't believe she broke up with me!"
Parent: "I guess you're hurt and ticked off, huh?"

Teen: "I'm never going to get these assignments done."
Parent: "Feeling like everything's piling up?"

•*Provide verbal and nonverbal feedback.* Make eye contact with your child. Show him you understand by nodding your head, maintaining an upright posture, and, if appropriate, interjecting an occasional comment such as "I see" or "That's interesting." Your child will pick up on your listening, and he'll be encouraged to keep talking. If he gets no responses, he may think you aren't interested. In that case, he'll pull back.

Some parents don't understand why their children do not talk with them, yet they give their children no reason to strike up a conversation. Years ago I watched a video presentation by Tom Peters. One segment featured a well-respected elementary school principal who obviously loved children. One way he showed respect for what the children had to say was that he never looked down at them while they were talking. He got down on his knees and looked them right in the eye. Maybe that is the first step for any of us who want to know our children better. Let's get down on their level and just . . . be quiet.

THINK AND TALK ABOUT IT

1. What instruction did James give about the relationship among speaking, listening, and anger? (1:19)
2. What will listening better do for you as a person? What will it do for your family?
3. Whom would you describe as a good listener? Why? Do you enjoy being with that person? Why?
4. What is the secret of effective listening?

Notes

1 Carl Smith, "How Can Parents Model Good Listening Skills?" (KidSource Online, Fall 1992, ERIC Clearinghouse on Reading and Communication Skills, Indiana University).

2 William Barclay, *Daily Study Bible-New Testament* (Louisville, KY: Westminster John Knox Press, 1975), Bible Explorer, Version 2.

3 Norman Wright and Rex Johnson, *Communication: Key to Your Teens* (Eugene, OR: Harvest House Publishers, 1978), 115-116.

4 Stephen R. Covey, *The 7 Habits of Highly Effective People* (New York: Simon and Schuster, 1990), 239-240.

5 Ibid., 241.

Chapter 7

TRUSTING ENOUGH
TO KNOW THEM

WE'D BEEN MARRIED A LITTLE OVER A YEAR and had just purchased our first house. We had a lot of work to do on it, but we were young and eager. I was going to be the master lawn-care specialist and I was so proud to mow my new lawn for the first time. When I finished, I grabbed a push broom and swept the driveway and walkway, satisfied with my accomplishments.

I need to give you one detail here: our walkways were not just plain concrete. The contractor had taken the time to put small scalloping decorations along the concrete path to the front door.

Not long after I finished the job, Pam came outside to survey my handiwork. "Well, what do you think?" I asked.

She looked right at the little sculpting details on the walkway and said, "Aren't you going to sweep the dirt out from the lines?"

I looked. "What dirt? I used the push broom on this."

Pam went into the garage, got the smaller broom, and began to sweep the dirt out of the cracks and scalloping.

Why did we see things so differently? It has to do with who we are—our basic temperaments. Looking back over our early years together, I can see that, had we understood the differences in our temperaments, we would have understood each other's frustrations on more than one similar occasion.

Thankfully, some years later, Pam and I took a course that changed all of this. I was working as an executive for a company that invited the wives to join the management team for a day-long seminar. We went into the San Bernardino National Forest, and for a whole day learned about ourselves.

We took a temperament test, and it changed our lives, our marriage, our social interactions, and our approach to child rearing. Up until this time, Pam and I had struggled with our differences. For example, Pam loves details, hence that dirt in the cracks was bothersome. I naturally focus on the big picture—a push broom represents the perfect tool for me. I just don't spend a lot of time on the details.

We've also applied the temperaments knowledge to our children. Our two children are very different from one another. And we learned that we couldn't "make them into our own images" because they were fundamentally different from us, as well. We realized, by studying the temperaments, that our children were not just extensions of our own personalities. They wouldn't naturally follow our example. We began to see that we would be quite wrong if we assumed that we commonly shared the same life experience—what each of us needed, wanted, thought, or felt. Paul Tournier said,

> *Our own personal experience can never be taken as the norm for other people. What matters is that our prayers should be living and sincere. Each of us has his own temperament; one is more intuitive, another more logical; one is more intellectual, another more emotional. The relationship of each with God will be marked with the stamp of his own particular temperament.[1]*

WHO ARE WE?

Yes, we're all "particular" individuals. Suppose we could recognize the different characteristics, or temperaments, of our children and clearly see how our own temperament integrates with theirs? If we can sort out the differences and understand why our children respond the way they do, we'll be able to TRUST enough to know them—and not FEAR when they respond in a way that's driven by their temperaments. So in the rest of this chapter, let's focus on understanding *who we are* and *why we do what we do.*

We're Wired Creatures

Temperaments are God's gift to us. God formed us for His good pleasure, and He wired each of us with a set of "operating instructions." One temperament isn't superior to another, just as spiritual gifts aren't a matter of superiority or inferiority. After all, it would be a wacky world if we were all alike, with similar responses and tastes. God gave us temperaments, talents, and spiritual gifts as a way to balance us in His Kingdom. "For he knoweth our frame" (Ps. 103:14).

He knows how we are made because He made us. Our make and build, our physical nature and temperament, our weaknesses and most tormenting temptations—He knows them all, for He searches our inmost nature. "He remembereth that we are dust," says the Bible. Made of dust, dust still, and ready to return to dust. We too often forget that we are dust. We place upon ourselves the stress of intellectual and physical extremes, but our Father never overloads us. He never fails to give us strength equal to our day, because He always considers our continual maturation.

I'm saying all of this simply to make a critical point: *Temperament is based upon the raw materials with which we were born.* God formed us in His image and gave each of us a little of this and a little of that. He chooses the various combinations and sets us on earth to love and serve Him. Therefore, we must allow for the work of the Holy Spirit within us. Each of us has weaknesses and areas of need within our personality and makeup. Through prayer, Bible Study, accountability within the church, and mentors we can experience change and growth through the work of the Holy Spirit.

One thing to keep in mind here: a child's physical condition can modify his or her temperament. Certain physical challenges can change a child's temperament (or mask it temporarily). Physical challenges demand careful attention from parents. At fourteen, I suffered a terrible knee injury. The injury took away my ability to play sports for almost two years, and consequently I gained fifty pounds. This event changed my temperament for many years. In light of my experience, I've learned that one of the greatest things a parent can do for their children is to provide an environment of love and understanding where the children are free to be themselves—even when they are depressed, angry, frustrated by the tough challenges of life.

We're Living Souls

A human being isn't just a bunch of parts formed together to make something unique. God doesn't have a workshop where He collects spare parts and suddenly assembles a human! He took body and spirit and created something very special, and no two are just alike.

The Lord breathed life into the human at Creation, and this being became a living soul out of the dust. Remember that it took God's breath to ignite life. According to the Holman Bible Dictionary,

> *The human being is a totality of being, not a combination of various parts and impulses. According to the Old Testament understanding, a person is not a body that happens to possess a soul. Instead, a person is a living soul. Genesis 2:7 relates God forming man 'of dust from the ground' and breathing into his nostrils 'the breath of life.'*[2]

Because of God's activity, humanity became a special and unique part of creation, "a living being." A person, thus, is a complete unit, made up of human flesh, spirit (we might call it "the lifeforce"), and *nephesh* (that is, "the total self," though it can be translated as "soul"). In other words, our bodily flesh can't exist by itself. Nor can spirit or *nephesh* exist by itself. Together, however, they make up a complete person.[3]

We're a Pretty Good "Likeness"

In the very beginning of the Bible, humans are depicted as the crowning center of God's creative activity, fearfully and wonderfully made. The verses say that everything God made is good. Humans, however are seen as very good. We are the centerpiece of God's creation.

> *26 Then God said, "Let us make man in our image, in our likeness, and let them rule over the fish of the sea and the birds of the air, over the livestock, over all the earth, and over all the creatures that move along the ground.". . .*
> *31 God saw all that he had made, and it was very good. And there was evening, and there was morning—the sixth day.*
> —Genesis 1:26-31 (NIV)

The creation is not only good, but the Creator thoroughly knows the created because God created humans in His image. The word "image" is the Hebrew *selem* and means "statue." In a sense, God is the eternal sculptor, taking formless clay and forming us into the statues He envisions for us to become.

1 This is the written account of Adam's line. When God created man, he made him in the likeness of God.
2 He created them male and female at the time they were created, he blessed them and called them "man."
3 When Adam had lived 130 years, he had a son in his own likeness, in his own image; and he named him Seth.
—Genesis 5:1-3 (NIV)

God created, blessed, and called them. The word translated "called" connotes a proclamation directed at a specific recipient for a specific purpose. God created human beings in His image for a specific purpose. God created temperaments so humans could have unique qualities and traits for different facets of God's ultimate plan.

1 Then God blessed Noah and his sons, saying to them, "Be fruitful and increase in number and fill the earth.
2 The fear and dread of you will fall upon all the beasts of the earth and all the birds of the air, upon every creature that moves along the ground, and upon all the fish of the sea; they are given into your hands.
3 Everything that lives and moves will be food for you. Just as I gave you the green plants, I now give you everything.
4 "But you must not eat meat that has its lifeblood still in it.
5 And for your lifeblood I will surely demand an accounting. I will demand an accounting from every animal. And from each man, too, I will demand an accounting for the life of his fellow man.
6 "Whoever sheds the blood of man, by man shall his blood be shed; for in the image of God has God made man.
7 As for you, be fruitful and increase in number; multiply on the earth and increase upon it."
—Genesis 9:1-7 (NIV)

This passage portrays the early stages of the life of Noah. Pay particular attention to verse 6. God is making humanity accountable. God is saying that he will demand an accounting if someone harms another human. Why would He do this? Because the human is made in His image. Life is precious, *and part of the precious life created by God is a person's temperament.* In Mark 12:16-17, Jesus has another encounter with Jewish leadership. They show him a coin and ask him a leading question about the image on it.

> *God's image in us means that we belong to him. The Pharisees and Herodians thought they had the perfect question to trap Jesus. However, Jesus answered wisely, once again exposing their self-interest and wrong motives. Jesus said that the coin bearing the emperor's image should be given to the emperor. However, our life, which bears God's image, belongs to God.*[4]

Tim LaHaye in his classic book, *Transformed Temperaments,* points out a number of harmful misconceptions about temperaments. If we consider the above Scriptures, it becomes obvious that we should not FEAR temperaments, but rather see them as a part of God's creation and plan. God, in His wisdom, gave each of us strengths and weaknesses. He gave us individual personality blueprints that should garner respect instead of worry. He designed them, and we should appreciate His creation.

WHY DO WE DO WHAT WE DO?

Remember the Old Testament Joseph? Like many young men of his day, he wanted more than he had. The young son of a farmer (who had twelve sons), Joseph was a dreamer. One day, he dreamed that he was lord and master and that his brothers and father would need to come to him for help. He made an almost fatal mistake at that point: he decided to tell his brothers about his dream. Their reaction? They tried to kill him and finally sold him as a slave to some desert travelers.

Let's consider his story from the perspective of understanding the temperaments. Note that Joseph didn't take the time to understand his family. He thought they'd be excited about his dream, just

The top misconceptions are:	
• One type is better than another.	• Response: No! God made us for His good pleasure, even though people tend to want to be something they are not.
• The whole system puts people in boxes.	• Response: God created temperaments for us to have different strengths or weaknesses. A temperament name is no different from any name. It simply is a way to help a person understand weaknesses, strengths, and why we respond the way we do.
• Temperament "guessing" can become a habit.	• Response: Yes, it can if not correctly controlled by the Holy Spirit's leading. Temperament training, and use for training, is like any tool: it can be misused.

as he was. Maybe he even thought the dream was funny, but they didn't share in the humor. In other words, he made a big mistake by not taking the time to understand fully the temperaments of his family (his audience).

We often make a similar mistake. We don't fully understand our family members. We take them for granted, or we simply try to push our ideas down their throats until they revolt. On the other hand, we also fail to see why they do communicate with us or include us. Many times we simply don't take the time (and it can be time consuming!) to understand them and their needs.

How, then, do we gain a better understanding of our family members, especially our children?

Understanding the Temperaments

Understanding comes from fully perceiving their temperaments and our temperament, as well. Parents also need to understand their children's needs and how to "read" the different temperaments' behavioral styles.

We must realize that each child is born with a specific personality direction. Our job as parents is to find it so that we can help them identify their strengths and choose careers that will fit their skills versus our desires. We can show them early in life where their weaknesses tend to be and how to avoid the pitfalls of their personality. When we function with the awareness of their inborn traits, we can then nurture them in the right direction. . . . Knowing the personalities can make such a positive change in a family.[5]

Specifically, how will this focus on temperaments help us become better parents? Consider two key "helpers" . . .

• *Help for Understanding Your Childrens' Needs.* Understanding the temperaments can help us better understand our children's needs. The single biggest obstacle to effective family communication is the tension that builds between parent and child. When tension is up, trust and cooperation are down. Conversely, when tension is down, cooperation and trust are up.

Take a moment to think through how you like to be treated. Chances are, if you're working with someone who is just like you, you'll do fine. However, if the other person is not like you, then you may have a problem, because he or she may not like to treat people the way you want to be treated. He or she may not communicate in your "style," may not move fast enough, or may move too fast. For example, if you're a quick and direct person who likes to get right to the point, and you approach someone who is a somewhat shy person, you may very well scare the person away by your seemingly "pushy" behavior. However, in the other person's mind, you haven't spent enough time on the details; you come across as superficial.

When families are created, chances are their personalities or temperaments are not identical. So . . . who should do the adjusting? The parents or the children? The truth is, if you work hard to understand your children's motivations, needs, and temperaments, you allow them to remain in their comfort zone, and your chances of communicating and helping them are much greater.

Jennifer was our firstborn. She is a talker, a charmer, and loves people. Zachary came along and is quiet, reserved, and only speaks when he has carefully considered his words. These differences in our children demanded that we adjust and become flexible in how we communicated. Pam, used to Jennifer's stories and almost nonstop conversation, had to adjust to Zachary's silence. She had to learn techniques (which we will discuss later) that helped her adjust to her son's temperament.

• *Help for "Reading" Your Children.* Understanding the temperaments can help us pick up on what's really going on inside our kids. Communication includes all the messages coming and going between parties. To effectively serve children, parents must start reading their children and determine how the children want to be approached. The good news is that your kids will teach you how to work with them if you pay attention to the messages they're sending.

Of all the people you meet on a daily basis, 75 percent are very different from you—they use time differently, make decisions differently, prefer to relate in different ways, and have a different style of communication. Part of the problem is that we assume that others will react to situations as we would ourselves. However, since three-quarters of the population is different from us, that's highly unlikely. Someone once said, "Learning is acquired by reading books, but the much more necessary learning . . . is only acquired by reading people, and studying all the various editions of them."

E.L. Thorndike, the pioneering American psychologist and educator, distinguished social intelligence from two other forms of intelligence—abstract and mechanical. His definition of social intelligence specifies two components: (1) The ability to understand others, and (2) the ability to act wisely in interpersonal situations.[6] These qualities are vital to effective child knowledge and care. Parents need to have the ability to understand their children and then act wisely in the interpersonal situations that develop. Many parents FEAR really getting involved deeply enough to understand their children. The next section will give you a tool to accomplish better understanding, or at least to discern temperament.

Before we begin an analysis of temperaments, I need to point out that there are several ways in which to discern a child's (or your own) temperament. Numerous books have been written on the subject, and most of them offer easy-to-use tests. *Personality Plus*, by Florence Littauer, is one of the most popular. Tim LaHaye has written several books on the subject, and this volume relies heavily on concepts he presents in *Transformed Temperaments*.[7] Both of these authors offer solid, Bible-based studies on temperaments as well as easy tests to understand your temperament. David Keirsey has written a new book titled *Please Understand Me II*. It offers a good analysis of the subject from a nonbiblical point of view. (He also has a website—http://www.keirsey.com—that features a temperament test. I found the test to be easy, but the information slightly different from Littauer's or LaHaye's.

On a more advanced level, there is an evaluation tool referred to as a DISC test. The Performax Company in Atlanta manages it. A person needs to be certified in order to administer this test, but someone in your local area may have the capability of helping you. This is an excellent tool for understanding the temperaments. Also, consider taking the Myers-Briggs Temperament Analysis. It's available from several sources and has an accompanying book that you can order from most book retailers. Like the DISC, Myers-Briggs is a comprehensive temperament tool.

The tool offered in this chapter is a simple, yet effective way for you to discern and understand temperaments. If you have not done so for yourself, why not look at the information and develop a profile of yourself before you begin analyzing your children? Have your mate or a close friend help you so you can have a more complete understanding of who you are and how God has made you. Then move to your children. Keep in mind there are no right or wrong answers with temperament tests. Honest answers are important, but no temperament is better than another. God made us just the way He wants us.

Recognizing Direct and Indirect Behavior

One way to recognize how children want to be approached is by observing the level of directness in their behavior. There's a marked difference between direct and indirect behavior. On a scale from direct to indirect, very direct people seek to control circumstances, information, or other people by taking charge of the situation. Indirect people prefer a slower, easier going pace. They're more tactful and will carefully consider options before actions.

In analyzing your children, one important component becomes a matter of where they would fit on a scale of direct and indirect behavior. The following table will give you guidelines for analyzing direct and indirect behavior:

INDIRECT	DIRECT
Approaches risk, decisions, or change slowly and cautiously	Approaches risk, decisions, or change quickly and spontaneously
Infrequent contributor to group conversations	Frequent contributor to group conversations
Infrequently uses gestures and voice intonation to emphasize points	Frequently uses gestures and voice intonation to emphasize points
Often makes qualified statements: "According to my sources . . ." , "I think so"	Often makes emphatic statements, "This is so!", "I'm positive!"
Emphasizes points through explanation of the content of the message	Emphasizes points through confident vocal intonation and assertive body language
Questions tend to be for clarification, support, or information	Questions tend to be rhetorical, to emphasize points or to challenge information
Reserves expression of opinions	Expresses opinions readily
More patient and cooperative	Less patient
Diplomatic; collaborative	Competitive, confronting, controlling
When not in agreement (if it's no big deal), most likely to go along	Most likely to maintain position when not in agreement (argues)
Understated; reserved	Intense; assertive
Initial eye contact is intermittent	Initial eye contact is sustained
At social gatherings, more likely to wait for others to introduce themselves	Most likely to introduce self to others at social gatherings
Gentle handshake	Firm handshake
Tends to follow established rules and policies	Tends to break or bend established rules and policies
Slow and deliberate movements	More rapid movements
Slow speech	Speaks more quickly, more intensely, and often more loudly
"Ask oriented"	"Tell oriented"[8]

As parents, we need to put our children on a scale from Indirect to Direct and observe their behavior in light of the two lists above.

Two other factors need to enter parents' thinking as they seek to understand their children's temperament. It is the difference between open and self-contained behavior.

OPEN	SELF-CONTAINED
Self-disclosing	Guarded
Shows and shares feelings freely	Keeps feelings private: shares only on a "need to know" basis
Makes most decisions based upon feelings (subjective)	Makes most decisions based upon evidence (objective)
Conversation includes digressions; strays from subject	Focuses conversation on issues and tasks; stays on subject
More relaxed and warm	More formal and proper
Goes with the flow	Goes with the agenda
Opinion-oriented	Fact-oriented
Easy to get to know in business or unfamiliar circumstances	Takes time to get to know in business or unfamiliar social situations
Approaches risk, decisions, or change slowly or cautiously	Primarily task-oriented
Flexible about how time is used	Disciplined about how time is used
Feels cramped by schedules	Prefers following an established schedule
Flexible expectations about people and situations	Fixed expectations about people and situations
Prefers to work with others	Prefers to work independently
Initiates or accepts physical contact	Avoids or minimizes physical contact
Shares or enjoys listening to personal feelings, especially if positive	Tells or enjoys listening to goal-related stories
Animated facial expressions during conversation	More likely to be expressionless during conversation
Shows more enthusiasm than the average person	Shows less enthusiasm than the average person
Friendly handshake	Formal handshake
More likely to give nonverbal feedback	Less likely to give nonverbal feedback
Responsive to dreams, visions, and concepts	Responsive to realities, actual experiences, facts; not interested in small talk
Loves to have fun	Wants power[9]

Using the preceding information, next plot where the child would be between open and self contained.

(RELATIONSHIP-ORIENTED)
OPEN

The Relater We're all in this together so let's work as a team.	The Socializer Let me tell you what happened to me.

INDIRECT   DIRECT
(SLOW PACE)   (FAST PACE)

The Thinker Can you provide documentation for your claims?	The Director I want it done right and I want it now.

SELF-CONTAINED
(TASK-ORIENTED)

When you combine directness with openness on a grid, the four quadrants represent the four basic behavioral styles. This combination creates four patterns or styles of behavior:

•Relater, Amiable, Phlegmatic (Cooperative, supportive, diplomatic, patient, loyal)	•Socializer, Expressive, Sanguine (Outgoing, enthusiastic, persuasive, fun- loving, spontaneous)
•Thinker, Analytical, Melancholy (Logical, thorough, serious, systematic, prudent)	•Director, Driver, Choleric (Independent, candid, decisive, pragmatic, efficient)

I hope you're beginning to recognize the great value of reading your children and understanding "where they're coming from" because of their temperaments. In the next chapter, we'll get a little more specific about how to apply it all to everyday life in your home.

THINK AND TALK ABOUT IT

1. What is your temperament?
2. How would you describe the temperaments of your children? What adjustments might you need to make as you compare your temperament to your children's?
3. How could you encourage your children to understand them selves and how God has made them?
4. What impact does understanding the temperaments have on your life? Your family?

Notes

1 Edythe Draper, *Draper's Book of Quotations*, #2818.

2 *Holman Bible Dictionary*, Electronic text and markup, © Epiphany Software, 1995.

3 Ibid.

4 *The Handbook of Bible Application* (Wheaton, IL: Tyndale House Publishers, Inc.) and WORDsearch Bible Study Software © 1987-1998, NavPress Software.

5 Florence Littauer, *Dare to Dream* (Dallas: Word Publishing, 1991), 80-81.

6 Paraphrased from Edward L. Thorndike, "Intelligence and Its Use," *Harper's*, 1920, 227-235.

7 Tim LaHaye, *Transformed Temperaments* (Wheaton, IL: Tyndale House Publishers, 1971).

8 Jim Cathcart, *Relationship Selling: How to Get and Keep Customers* (HDL Publishing, 1988), 22.

9 Ibid., 26.

Chapter 8

TRUSTING ENOUGH TO UNDERSTAND THEM

OVER 2,000 YEARS AGO HIPPOCRATES CREATED a system of categorizing what he called the four basic temperaments. As we saw in the previous chapter, there are a variety of temperament tools available to us; however, most of them have their roots in the work of Hippocrates. Here's a description-at-a-glance of his categories with reference to some of our recent Presidents.

Hippocrates	Description	Our Term	Presidential Example
Sanguine	Magnetic Personality	Socializer	Reagan
Choleric	Commanding Personality	Director	Nixon
Melancholy	Analytical Personality	Thinker	Carter
Phlegmatic	Pleasing Personality	Relater	Ford[1]

What hope there is in relating well to others when we understand the temperaments! In this chapter we will look at strengths and weaknesses in each of these temperaments and learn how we can encourage the development of our children's strengths while helping them control their weaknesses.

We'll also look at some Bible "heroes" to see how their temperaments were used in the Lord's service. But first let's pause here to remind ourselves that all of us have strengths and weaknesses. Many parents spend so much time on the weaknesses, however, that they forget the strengths. Weaknesses are simply *strengths taken to their extreme.* Our daughter Jennifer has a wonderful, engaging personality. I've often said she could charm the bark from a tree. Her weakness? When her strength—being with and influencing people—is taken to its extreme, she can become too chatty. She also tries to please people too much. Our son, Zachary, is quite the opposite. He's a reflective thinker and likes being immersed in the details. His weakness? He can get lost in over-analysis of the minutia—failing to see the forest because of all the trees in his way!

We parents need to understand, and work with, both the strengths and weaknesses. That way we're allowing the Holy Spirit to do His work in our children, just as they are. Nevertheless, we can keep encouraging our children to function in the areas of their strengths. For example, if I were to ask Jennifer to focus all her attention on details, especially on numbers, she wouldn't be happy. On the other hand, if I asked Zachary to lead a social committee, he'd hardly be thrilled. Both need the freedom to work and serve in the areas of their strengths.

It was the same with the people of the Bible. As we look at four biblical personalities, we can't cover every weakness or strength. But drawing from Tim LaHaye's classic book *Transformed Temperaments,* I want to highlight a few of each so any of us can better identify our children and see how their temperaments can be used for God's glory.

Peter the Socializer

Everybody loves the Apostle Peter. He's loved for many reasons, but one of the most powerful is that his shortcomings are out in the open for everybody to see. He was the one who always spoke out of turn, often without thinking first. He took dynamic action in the Garden when Jesus was being arrested. In so many instances, this apostle landed right in the middle of the action, surrounded by lots of people. And why not? He was clearly a Socializer. Consider:

• *Peter was impulsive.* Matthew 4:20 says, "they straightway left their nets, and followed him." Peter didn't give it any thought; he just went with Jesus. And that involved some pretty risky following: Peter even tries his hand at walking on water! Did he stop to analyze first? No, he had a destination in mind; the details of how to get there could be left to someone else.

A common tendency of the Socializer (sanguine) is to "leap before looking and then tremble at the possible consequences."[2] Socializers are usually the first to volunteer and then later regret the decision. They are the first to speak but usually haven't put a lot of thought into what they're saying.

•*Peter was inconsistent.* Most Socializers live life at the extremes. They can be way "up" one day and fall way down the next. They can erupt in anger or be silent and pouty. Their emotions are hot or cold; they're floating high as the clouds in the morning, sinking low into the cellar by evening. Or vice versa! Thankfully, as Peter launched into his ministry, he was filled with the Holy Spirit and became a much more even-tempered person. By God's grace he was able to overcome the pitfalls of a Socializer temperament.

LaHaye points out that the Lord Jesus saw this in Peter and acted. Jesus changed Peter's name from Simon to Peter ("rock"). Instead of giving him a new name like "hot head" or "gabby," Jesus chose a name that reflected the character Peter *could become under the control of the Holy Spirit.* That is the goal for our children too. Parents who tease their kids about temperament issues should use Jesus as a model. He chose a name that reflected the good side of Peter—and all the potential within him—instead of a name that reflected what he would become if he didn't change.

•*Peter was enthusiastic.* When John, James, and Peter had witnessed the transfiguration of Jesus, it was Peter who came bounding down from the mountaintop ready to go. "As the men were leaving Jesus, Peter said to him, 'Master, it is good for us to be here. Let us put up three shelters—one for you, one for Moses and one for Elijah.' (He did not know what he was saying)" (Luke 9:33, NIV). Peter was so impressed with what he saw, he just couldn't keep his excitement bottled up. He missed the point of this historic moment, but he was full of enthusiasm nonetheless.

Other traits of the Socializer temperament include:

The Extrovert	The Talker	The Optimist
Good sense of humor	Memory for color	Curious
Appealing personality	Enthusiastic and expressive	Charming
Volunteers for jobs	Inspiring	Turns disaster into humor

Paul the Director

Paul is the best scriptural example of the Director (or choleric) temperament. What is amazing about Paul is how the Spirit worked in him to soften the usual hard edges found in this temperament. However, as you read the New Testament accounts of Paul, you can easily see his Director style coming through.

• *Paul was strong-willed.* Both the Director and the Thinker have elements of a strong will about them. The Director focuses on determination. When pointed in the right direction, this can be a powerful force for good. When pointed in the wrong direction, it can lead to excessive control and a "never say die" attitude that may push well past reason.

> *24 Do you not know that in a race all the runners run, but only one gets the prize? Run in such a way as to get the prize.*
>
> *25 Everyone who competes in the games goes into strict training. They do it to get a crown that will not last; but we do it to get a crown that will last forever.*
>
> *26 Therefore I do not run like a man running aimlessly; I do not fight like a man beating the air.*
>
> *27 No, I beat my body and make it my slave so that after I've preached to others, I myself will not be disqualified for the prize.*
>
> —1 Corinthians 9:24-27 (NIV)

This text reveals much about the strong-willed Director Paul. First is the intense desire to reach the goal. Paul didn't want any distractions, and he was tenacious in his efforts to win the prize. Directors need to be careful that they don't mow others down in their efforts to succeed. Clearly, Paul didn't run aimlessly. Directors seldom stop to smell the roses. They see the prize, sense the competition, and set their whole being toward achievement. For many directors, the achieving process is more important than the reward at the end. Peter would have been concerned about the reward and the accolades; Paul was only concerned about getting there and staying on course. Everything Directors do has meaning and purpose. They work themselves out of trouble. They oftentimes substitute work for expressing emotions and showing feelings.

Paul was self-sufficient. The Director relies on himself for meeting any problem or emergency. He has a difficult time trusting anyone, including God, for help. Paul was a Spirit-filled Christian as he learned to trust others and delegate his ministry tasks. God showed him a better way, but it took Paul a long time to see the benefits of letting others help.

I believe that early in Paul's ministry, when he went into the desert to be alone, he was living out his Director style. He had to learn by himself, trusting no one to help him with his newfound faith. His words in Acts 20:34-35 (NIV) also show Paul's self-sufficiency:

> *You yourselves know that these hands of mine have supplied my own needs and the needs of my companions. In everything I did, I showed you that by this kind of hard work we must help the weak, remembering the words the Lord Jesus himself said: "It is more blessed to give than to receive."*

He was an independent contractor, an entrepreneurial tent maker, beholden to no one for his living wages. He stressed hard work to get the "job"—helping the weak—done. A person with a different temperament might have thought of compassion for the weak; Paul thought of *problem-solving* for them.

Paul was dynamic and bold. Directors are often dynamic personalities. Especially when their second tendency is the Socializer. Former presidents Ronald Reagan, Franklin Roosevelt, John Kennedy, and Lyndon Johnson all were Director/Socializers. Like these men, Paul emerged as an influential leader. Though he began as the "new Christian," he eventually emerged as leader of all.

He boldly preached the Gospel everywhere he went, planting churches wherever he could. In Rome, Paul witnessed to his captors and kept in touch with the local churches through dynamic letters. Paul never let his time slip away, but rather witnessed fearlessly to anyone who would listen.

Other traits of the Director temperament include:

The Extrovert	The Doer	The Optimist
Born leader	Must correct wrongs	Goal-oriented
Confident	Little need for friends	Dynamic and active
Practical decision-making	Independent	Unemotional

Moses the Thinker

Moses, the great leader of the Exodus, had a Thinker, or Melancholy temperament. He possessed a brilliant mind that wanted to be involved in every detail. Yet he also gave in to the Thinker's propensity to allow negative thoughts to control his judgment. Thinkers can be perfectionists, yet they are sensitive to others' needs, making them self-sacrificing and extremely loyal.

• *Moses was gifted.* Tim LaHaye writes, "The inherent talent and gifts of Moses the Melancholy are apparent throughout the entire scriptural narrative. In Acts 7, Stephen, the first Christian martyr, informs us that Moses "was learned in all the wisdom of the Egyptians, and was mighty in words and deeds" (v. 22).[3] Moses had tremendous abilities to care for over three million people roaming the desert. He was able to think through all the details necessary for such an expedition. He was also the perfect leader who would trust God for every need. Unlike the Director, Moses the Thinker wouldn't look to himself for leadership, but he would gather facts and think through what needed to be done. His gifted nature gave him the ability to seek God at every turn.

• *Moses was depressed*. According to LaHaye, only Elijah and Jonah show the emotional lows equal to Moses. Thinkers can be gracious in appearance, yet hurting deeply on the inside. Their lows are much lower than any of the other four basic temperaments. Numbers 11:10-15 (NIV) shows Moses at a low point:

> 10 Moses heard the people of every family wailing, each at the entrance to his tent. The LORD became exceedingly angry, and Moses was troubled.
> 11 He asked the LORD, "Why have you brought this trouble on your servant? What have I done to displease you that you put the burden of all these people on me?
> 12 Did I conceive all these people? Did I give them birth? Why do you tell me to carry them in my arms, as a nurse

carries an infant, to the land you promised on oath to their forefathers?
13 Where can I get meat for all these people? They keep wailing to me, 'Give us meat to eat!'
14 I cannot carry all these people by myself; the burden is too heavy for me.
15 If this is how you are going to treat me, put me to death right now—if I have found favor in your eyes—and do not let me face my own ruin."

Where Paul would have thought he could have carried all the people by himself, Moses slips into a deep depression. In fact, Moses is so depressed that he speaks disparagingly of God and His provision. Paul would have dynamically confronted the people as well; however, Moses chose to whine and complain, slipping into negative thinking. Paul would have fought; Moses wanted to die or run away.

This verse shows a great contrast between the temperaments. Directors and Socializers are fighters. They look at obstacles, and their first response is combative. Thinkers and Relaters prefer flight. Like Moses who wanted to die, Thinkers and Relaters would rather "just pull the covers over their heads" instead of directly attacking a problem or burden.

President Jimmy Carter's reelection campaign in 1980 provides a great example of this temperament truth. Carter was a Thinker, a brilliant nuclear physicist; however; his White House experience largely depressed him. When he ran for reelection, he came under great criticism for the Iranian hostage situation. What did he choose to do? He staged the famous Rose Garden campaign. He didn't attack his critics; he stayed home. Ronald Reagan, instead, went on the offensive and eventually won the campaign. Carter chose flight, while Reagan (a Director/Socializer) chose to fight.

•*Moses was a perfectionist.* Moses was the man of the Law. The details of the Law, which he wrote under God's direction, would exhaust anyone of another temperament. Moses, however, was the right man for this task. He enjoyed putting together the intricate laws of the Hebrews, even though his bent toward perfectionism almost killed him!

> 13 The next day Moses took his seat to serve as judge for the
> people, and they stood around him from morning till
> evening.
> 14 When his father-in-law saw all that Moses was doing
> for the people, he said, "What is this you are doing for the
> people? Why do you alone sit as judge, while all these peo-
> ple stand around you from morning till evening?"
> 15 Moses answered him, "Because the people come to me
> to seek God's will.
> 16 Whenever they have a dispute, it is brought to me, and
> I decide between the parties and inform them of God's
> decrees and laws."
> 17 Moses' father-in-law replied, "What you are doing is
> not good.
> 18 You and these people who come to you will only wear
> yourselves out. The work is too heavy for you; you cannot
> handle it alone."
> —Exodus 18:13-18 (NIV)

Moses was so into the details that he couldn't delegate. He
feared, like most perfectionists, that no one else could do the job as
well as he could. Where the Socializer would enlist others to help,
and the Director would tell others what to do, Moses the Thinker
could only envision doing it all himself. It took wise counsel from
Jethro, his father-in-law, to get Moses to think about an alternative—
choosing other capable men to handle some of the work. Many
Christian leaders have learned delegation from this section of the
Bible and Jethro's wise counsel.

• ***Moses was loyal.*** Melancholy/Thinkers are loyal and faithful,
great friends and trusted partners. This characteristic drove Moses to
a deep trust and love for God. He was loyal to God's plans (where
a Director would need to develop one of his own) in reaching
Pharaoh.

Thinkers do make wonderful friends. Their loyalty provides
folks of other temperaments with lifelong companions. "Because
Perfect Melancholies [Thinkers] are perfectionists, they want perfect
mates. They make friends cautiously, to see if people measure up,
and they would rather have a few faithful, devoted friends than an

abundance of acquaintances as do Popular Sanguines [Socializers]."[4]

Other traits of the Thinker temperament include:

The Introvert	The Thinker	The Pessimist
Deep and thoughtful	Analytical	Serious and purposeful
Genius tendencies	Sensitive to others	Sets high standards
Detail oriented	Idealistic	Self-sacrificing

Abraham the Relater

The easiest of all to get along with, Relaters have a calm spirit and easy-going manner. They enjoy dry humor, never show much emotion, and are in general a Mr. Nice Guy. Florence Littauer writes, "God did create peaceful phlegmatics [relaters] as special people to be buffers for the emotions of the other three [temperaments], to provide stability and balance."[5]

Abraham was peaceable. The Relater wants, above all, harmony and peace. Abraham shows his penchant for peace over possession in Genesis 13 when he suggests a compromise in the face of potential conflict.

8 Abram said to Lot, "Let's not have any quarreling between you and me, or between your herdsmen and mine, for we are brothers.
9 Is not the whole land before you? Let's part company. If you go to the left, I'll go to the right; if you go to the right, I'll go to the left."
— Genesis 13:8-9 (NIV)

Abram (at this point in his life) chose compromise instead of a fight. Where the Director would have wanted to argue, or the Thinker would have sought a way to plot, chart, count, or make a list, the Relater wants only to have a peaceful resolution—even if it means he'll lose something of his own. In the 1930s, British Prime Minister Chamberlain's famous quote, "Peace at any price," was highly Relater-like, as Hitler's troops were ready to storm all of Europe!

Abraham was reliable. Both Directors and Relaters have the ability to rise to the occasion. They do it differently, but they both can be heavily relied upon under pressure. (Note: Genesis 14 will give you an exciting example of Abraham's reliable strength under pressure.) Much of General Eisenhower's strength under the immense pressure of leading the troops in World War II can be traced to his Relater temperament. President George Bush's successful Desert Storm campaign had much to do with his ability to relate to other world leaders, under extreme pressure, and receive their full support.

Abraham was passive. This temperament trait got Abraham into great trouble with God. He lied to kings about his wife, and he let his wife's immediate need almost jeopardize his relationship with God. We read in Genesis 16 about Sarah's inability to conceive. She develops a plan to have a child out of her impatience and Abram, instead of thinking through the details, or confronting her with his true feelings . . . compromises. It's a sad piece of history with eventual long-term casualties.

In our family, Zachary is prone to compromise his own feelings or better judgments. When he and Jennifer used to play together, his passivity would allow Jennifer to plan his entire day. Later, when he'd had enough, he would get angry and storm away. However, it was his passive nature that got him into the mess in the first place.

Other traits of the Relater temperament include:

The Introvert	The Watcher	The Pessimist
Low-key personality	Relaxed, patient	Quiet
Humor mediates	Problem solver	Competent, steady
Good under pressure	Avoids conflicts	Consistent

Understanding Your Child's Reactions

After this short description of biblical personalities, what will make this exploration complete for you is to analyze your children's reactions to specific situations in light of their own personalities. As you do this in the days ahead, keep in mind our definition for weaknesses: *strengths taken to the extreme.* As you consider each child's temperament, carefully and gently explore areas for improvement and recognize that you can guide him or her to overcome them.

The following table will help you better understand each of the four basic temperaments:

	Relater	Thinker	Director	Socializer
Behavior Pattern	Open/Direct	Self-contained/ Indirect	Self-contained/ Direct	Open/Direct
Appearance	Casual Conforming	Formal Conservative	Businesslike Functional	Fashionable Stylish
Space	Personal Relaxed Friendly Informal	Structured Organized Functional Formal	Busy Formal Efficient Structured	Stimulating Personal Cluttered Friendly
Pace	Slow/Easy	Slow/Systematic	Fast/Decisive	Fast/Spontaneous
Priority	Maintaining relationships	The task: the process	The task: the results	Interacting in relationships
Fears	Confrontation	Embarrassment	Loss of Control	Loss of Prestige
Under Tension Will:	Submit/Acquiesce	Withdraw/Avoid	Dictate/Assert	Attack/Be Sarcastic
Seeks:	Attention	Accuracy	Productivity	Recognition
Needs to Know	How it will affect his personal circumstances	How it works	What is does, by when, what it costs	How it enhances his status, who else uses it
Gains Security by:	Close relationships	Preparation	Control	Flexibility
Wants to Maintain:	Relationships	Credibility	Success	Status
Support His/Her:	Feelings	Thoughts	Goals	Ideas
Achieves Acceptance by:	Conformity Loyalty	Correctness Thoroughness	Leadership Competition	Playfulness Entertaining
Likes You to Be:	Pleasant	Precise	To the point	Stimulating
Wants to Be:	Liked	Correct	In Charge	Admired
Irritated by:	Insensitivity Impatience	Surprises Unpredictability	Inefficiency Indecision	Inflexibility Routine
Measures Personal Worth by:	Compatibility with Others Depth of Relationships	Precision Accuracy Activity	Results Track Record Measurable Progress	Acknowledgement Recognition Applause
Decisions Are:	Considered	Deliberate	Definite	Spontaneous[6]

The chart on page 143 can help you understand your children in everyday situations. For example, if you notice that little Susie is slow getting ready for school, if she usually has a very casual appearance and a pleasant demeanor, chances are she's a Relater. If little Billy is slow, but quite systematic in how he does things, dresses conservatively, and wants everything precise, Billy is a Thinker.

This table is a tool for helping you to relate to your child in various situations. Depending on the event, you'll adjust your response as appropriate. However, if your child has a Director temperament, for example, the first thing you want to do is get to the point. In our family, we call it "getting to the bottom line." Many times, as Jennifer was growing up, we had to immediately get to the bottom line with her. We had to ferret out the high points, learn some facts (but not walk through every step), and quickly give her some options. We had to put the decision into her hands as soon as that was appropriate. We sought to help her save time and we tried to move quickly. Lectures never worked; she just didn't have the time or patience for them.

Now Zachary's needs were thoroughly different, calling for a contrasting approach from us. As he was growing up, we had to be prepared to walk him through every step with clear and detailed explanations. He seeks precise information, and we had to be accurate or he wouldn't accept what we were saying. He had to be sure of every detail in what we were saying, and we couldn't stray from the facts.

Increasing Your Behavioral Flexibility

Since each temperament has its underlying needs (refer back to the chart), parents, in order to relate best to their children, need to develop behavioral flexibility. This is the ability to adapt your own response or behaviors to meet the unique needs of your children. No, this isn't manipulation. You aren't trying to change your children, ridicule them, or make them into what you want them to be. You are merely trying to adapt to their basic approach to reality in order to relate and communicate more meaningfully. You are trying to find some common ground. Jim Cathcart refers to this as the platinum rule: "Do unto others as they would like to be done unto."[7]

Treating people the way they want to be treated frees up the relationship. It helps everyone get past temperamental differences and opens the lines of communication and trust. Changing to meet your children's needs allows them to remain in their comfort zone. You don't ask your children to become something they can't become; rather, you recognize their temperamental needs and respond accordingly. What a tension reducer!

Carl Sandburg told of the chameleon that lived very well, adjusting moment by moment to his environment, until one day he had to cross a Scotch plaid. He died at the crossroads, heroically trying to blend with all the colors at once.[8] We shouldn't try to be human chameleons, but we should do whatever we can to fully understand our children and ourselves so we can improve our relationships.

Remember that under stress most of us will revert to what is called a "backup style." We all experience stress at times. Usually, in the home, stress lingers around the corner as parents discipline children or as children grow and want to become more independent. It's important to know each temperament's backup style so when stress comes, we can be aware and adjust.

A person's primary backup style is her predictable, unconscious shift of behavior in response to stress. The backup style is usually counterproductive to resolving the situation and can cause some serious relationship damage. For example, the Apostle Paul's backup style surfaced in the incident with Barnabas and Mark. Paul became very dictatorial and would have lost a friend if Barnabas hadn't been such an encourager.

Each temperament has its own primary backup:

Director	autocratic
Socializer	attacking
Thinker	avoiding
Relater	acquiescing

•The Director becomes pushy and dictatorial. Her voice becomes level and intense. She is unyielding in her opinions. She focuses on the task and the work ahead.

•The Socializer gets angry and verbal. He employs strong lan-

guage and gestures. The volume of his voice greatly increases.
- The Thinker becomes the avoider. She'll get up and leave the argument rather than stay and fight.
- The Relater will just give in. He prefers compliance to cooperation. The classical passive/aggressive behavior could emerge in backup mode. He will do a task, but not the way you want it done, or in a timely way, etc.

Parents who TRUST need to break a vicious cycle here. For example, parents who are Socializers or Directors take note. If your child leaves the room during a disagreement, it may not be because she's trying to be disrespectful; she may just be a Thinker and want to avoid a confrontation.

The table on page 145, the short discussion on backup styles, and the next section on decreasing tension are here to help you learn to break the cycle. When parents begin to understand their children's temperaments and what motivates them in different situations, it serves to take the pressure off our family relationships. We can look at each other's different needs in a positive way and stop trying to make everyone be like us.

Breaking the cycle isn't a manipulative tactic, but rather an honest, sincere attempt to understand. It must be done with acceptance and true graciousness. Think of it for a moment. If you are a Director, trying to discipline a Director child, both of you naturally back up into an autocratic behavior pattern. The argument/discussion will go nowhere unless you, as a parent, break the cycle by recognizing your child's backup style and refusing to meet it with your own.

In this case, the parent needs to direct the conversation away from butting heads and look for ways to compromise. If both the parent and the child remain in the autocratic mode, nothing positive will come from the encounter. Only hurt feelings, anger, and continual frustration will result.

Doing these things is how we make it possible to live together in peace. Learning to live together, and TRUSTing enough to understand your children, involves three things: First, it's knowing the strengths and weaknesses of each other. Second, it's appreciating the strengths and weaknesses of each other. Third, it's practicing open communication.

20 There are many parts, but one body.
21 The eye cannot say to the hand, "I don't need you!" And
the head cannot say to the feet, "I don't need you!"
22 On the contrary, those parts of the body that seem to be
weaker are indispensable,
23 and the parts that we think are less honorable we treat
with special honor. And the parts that are unpresentable
are treated with special modesty,
24 while our presentable parts need no special treatment.
But God has combined the members of the body and has
given greater honor to the parts that lacked it,
25 so that there should be no division in the body, but that
its parts should have equal concern for each other.
—1 Corinthians 12:20-25 (NIV)

Paul is talking here about the parts of the physical body and comparing them to the church body. He is asking for unity. He is also calling for knowing and appreciating strengths and weaknesses. We can't TRUST enough to understand without fully understanding and appreciating the strengths and weaknesses of our child's temperament.

Zachary is very detail-oriented, methodical, and precise. He is also much better than I am at fixing things around the house. Early on, when I noticed his skill with mechanical gadgets, I let him fix things. At first I trusted him with the simple things; then as he grew up, he took on the more complex projects. By understanding his strengths, I could relate to him. And he wasn't frustrated, sitting back watching me struggle with an "easy" repair job.

29 Do not let any unwholesome talk come out of your
mouths, but only what is helpful for building others up
according to their needs, that it may benefit those who lis-
ten.
—Ephesians 4:29 (NIV)

The practice of open communication helps families learn to live together this way. Earlier I alluded to our evening devotionals. I firmly believe that the discussions during those times laid the foundation for us to practice open communication. We also realized that Jennifer would be the more vocal child and Zachary would be a man of few words. That was fine; it just meant that we'd develop techniques to lead him into discussion and to show Jennifer the great benefits of more listening.

Decreasing Your Tension-Causing Behavior
Every one of us has behavior patterns that can cause tension in others. The lists below can help you see how your temperament may "bother" your child and cause tension.

If you are a Director, what's bothersome . . .
- To other Directors—Your tendency to over-control a situation, reducing their own freedom and ability to control.
- To Socializers—Your concern for results, accompanied by an apparent lack of concern for a motivational or fun environment.
- To Relaters—Your tendency not to take enough time to listen; your tendency to put relationships low on the priority list.
- To Thinkers—Your being so quick to get the work done—but perhaps not thoroughly enough.

If you are a Socializer, what's bothersome . . .
- To other Socializers—Your desire for visibility, especially if it reduces their visibility.
- To Directors—Your apparent lack of a results orientation; being too emotional.
- To Relaters—Your lack of depth in some of your relationships, and your quickness.
- To Thinkers—Your lack of attention to detail; your impulsive tendencies.

If you are a Relater, what's bothersome . . .
- To other Relaters—Your lack of initiative, especially if it means they have to initiate.
- To Directors—Your tendency to engage in too much small talk.
- To Socializers—Your apparent lack of quickness.
- To Thinkers—Your people orientation; your tendency to spend "time in talk" over "time on task."

If you are a Thinker, what's bothersome . . .

- To other Thinkers—Your desire to be more right or correct than they are.
- To Directors—Your slower and more methodical pace.
- To Socializers—Your persistent attention to detail.
- To Relaters—Your lack of letting them know how you "feel."

The next chart will help you not only see what can irritate your children, but it can help you evaluate your children and how they can, again, learn to get along.

Taking the Next Steps

Use the table below as a tool for helping your children overcome certain temperamental weaknesses. Remember our definition of weakness is any strength taken to its extreme. Here are some ways for parents to take action, communicate, and coach.

Socializers	Thinkers	Relaters	Directors
Recognize their difficulty in accomplishing tasks	Know that they are very sensitive and get hurt easily	Realize they need direct motivation	Recognize they are born leaders
Realize they like variety and flexibility	Realize they are programmed with a pessimistic attitude	Help them to set goals and make rewards	Insist on two-way communication
Keep them from accepting more than they can do	Help them deal with depression	Don't expect enthusiasm	Know that they don't mean to hurt
Don't expect them to remember appointments or be on time	Compliment them sincerely and lovingly	Force them to make decisions	Try to divide areas of responsibility
Praise them for everything	Accept that they like it quiet sometimes	Don't heap all the blame on them	Realize they aren't compassionate[9]
Remember they are circumstantial people	Enjoy quiet	Encourage them to accept responsibilities	
Bring them presents; they like new toys	Try to keep a reasonable schedule		
Realize they mean well	Help them not to be the family's slave		

If you are a Director	If you are a Thinker	If you are a Socializer	If you are a Relater
Learn to listen, be patient	Develop focus on the right things, not just doing things right	Be less impulsive	Be less sensitive to what people think
Develop greater concern for people	Try to respond more quickly	Be more results oriented	Be more concerned with the task
Be more flexible with people	Trust your intuition	Control actions—be less demonstrative	Face confrontation
Be more supportive	Be less fact oriented	Focus attention on details and facts	Be more decisive
Explain "why"	Look ahead	Listen, don't talk so much	Increase pace
Be warmer. . . more open	Be more open and flexible	Slow down pace	Initiate and learn to say "no"

All this is meant to increase your family compatibility. By identifying your temperament, you can control how you respond. By identifying your children's temperaments, you can see how God made them and TRUST Him to help you encourage, respond, and build relationships with them. Don't FEAR complete understanding of your children's temperaments. Embrace this knowledge as an important step to TRUSTing enough to parent. The real benefit of TRUSTing comes from successfully meeting needs of the children. Galatians 6:2 says, "Carry each other's burdens, and in this way you will fulfill the law of Christ" (NIV). What a joy to carry the burdens of our children! What a delight to help them grow to love God!

THINK AND TALK ABOUT IT

1. List your strengths and weaknesses. What are your children's strengths and weaknesses?
2. List some ways you and your children can work together better.
3. Why did Paul make himself a slave to everyone? Why is it important for parents to learn how to communicate and relate to their children?
4. What would be the best way to use your unique abilities in your

family? What unique abilities do your children have that they are not using in the family?

Notes

1 Adapted from Florence Littauer's *Personalities in Power*.

2 Tim LaHaye, *Transformed Temperaments* (Wheaton, IL: Tyndale House Publishers, 1971), 33.

3 Ibid., 98.

4 Florence Littauer, *Personality Plus! How to Understand Others by Understanding Yourself* (Grand Rapids, MI: Fleming H. Revell, 1983), 55.

5 Ibid., 73.

6 Jim Cathcart, *Relationship Selling*, 27.

7 Ibid., 30.

8 This story came in a speech by Gene Bartlett.

9 This table is a compilation of ideas from several sources: *Personality Plus!* by Florence Littauer, *Social Style/Management Style*, by Robert and Dorothy Grover Boulton and *Relationship Selling*, by Jim Cathcart.

Chapter 9

TRUSTING ENOUGH TO CONFRONT

THE DUKE WAS ALWAYS THE TRUSTED, loyal fighting man who took control in every conflict. Oh, he'd stay pretty calm as the action unfolded, but we knew the big fight was coming. The inevitable showdown: John Wayne against the evil enemy, the greedy rancher, the aggressor army. Usually it happened near the end of the movie, the big man walking up the street or through the jungle, eyes narrowed and focused. Then Wayne stops, pulls his guns, and . . . bang! bang!—it's all over.

The grim warrior walks away, savoring the victory.

Or maybe you're more the classic TV fan. In that case, you'll no doubt recall the heroics of Matt Dillon on *Gunsmoke*. The small-town marshall was typically out of town while the rest of the characters got themselves into a heap of trouble, or somebody would come into town and cause all kinds of havoc and destruction. Then, at the very end, Dillon would appear. He'd draw his guns, settle the dispute, make the world a safe place once again. Matt confronted the evil, and it was gone. Not many did it better.

Except maybe Ward Cleaver or Mike Brady. No, these men weren't gunslinging sheriffs or World War II heroes; they were just fathers. Ward led the family in *Leave It to Beaver*, Mike Brady was the father in the blended family of *The Brady Bunch*. Both men (one from the '50s and one from the '70s) were the made-for-TV conflict specialists. In different styles, they led their families to safety and security. Ward had his den, where he'd impart gems of wisdom to the Beaver or Wally; Mike often faced chaos in the household, but he usually took a moment, at the end of the show, to make sense of it all. Mike's style was looser (reflecting the values of his generation), but nonetheless he got the job done. Like John Wayne or Matt Dillon, he pulled his "guns" and ended the trouble for the Brady house.

In light of your film and television-viewing history, consider what you've been taught about confrontation. Is it that someone else (the quiet stranger) will come into your "town" and straighten up the mess (maybe by blowing things away)? Or is it that someone within your family or group was wiser or better and would clean everything up? Or that at the end of every conflict "episode" a major dialogue would happen and, as a result, you'd live happily ever after?

So many of the old fictional characters portrayed conflict and confrontation as things that brew like tea until they reach a boiling point. In such cases, the confrontation usually leads to a blowup. Things progress from bad to worse to absolutely terrible, before somebody comes forward and makes some sense of the matter and straightens things out.

Here's my point: *real confrontation isn't as we've been taught* in the movies or on television. Confrontation is a skill that parents need to develop in order to discipline and teach their children. Confrontation is a natural step from listening better and understanding temperaments. Once parents begin to listen, they hear needs (or opinions) expressed by their children. Once needs are expressed (and fully understood), the parents will look at those needs in light of who their children are, how they were made by God. This understanding may lead to the necessity to confront a child, not waiting until it is too late and a blowup occurs. Not waiting for someone (or some thing like school or church) to come along and do it for them. Not even waiting until God grants them perfect wisdom and knowledge.

Confrontation may need to happen right now. I know it's easier to allow FEAR to control us rather than TRUSTing God to help us confront our children, yet confrontation ought to be a natural part of child rearing. Sadly, the mass media has taught us that it is always an explosive thing, an excruciating task, something to be avoided. It's too bad that many parents have bought into this stereotype, because effective confrontation can lead to growth, discernment, and maturity in children.

DO YOU CARE ENOUGH TO CONFRONT?

On a recent tour of a local major bookstore, I was amazed to see how many parenting books ignore the topic of confrontation. I found that most dispense information on what parents can do "to" their children, rather than the positive outcomes caused by actions parents do "with" their children. I picked up dozens of books by recognized experts, but for some reason they chose not to discuss confrontation.

Next, I went to the Internet and searched for "children and confrontation." Again I was amazed at the lack of available research. It seems we will confront anything today—except our children. We will confront crime, AIDS, addictions, civil authority, prejudice, terrorism, racism, tobacco. But we choose not to confront our children.

The Scriptures teach quite the opposite, offering excellent examples of good confrontation and its positive benefits. God Himself confronts His people and cares enough about their daily lives to send a "helper" to confront us. When Jesus faced problems, He tackled them head-on. He didn't wait for the closing scene, the dramatic buildup. He moved forward in His relationships, with friends and enemies, by confronting and giving us a supreme model from which to learn.

The biblical accounts reviewed in this chapter should serve to convince any parent that confrontation is the right thing to do in relationships. The final account shows the disasters of not confronting.

Paul Confronts Peter

11 When Peter came to Antioch, I opposed him to his face, because he was in the wrong.
12 Before certain men came from James, he used to eat with the Gentiles. But when they arrived, he began to draw back and separate himself from the Gentiles because he was afraid of those who belonged to the circumcision group.
—Galatians 2:11-12 (NIV)

Paul the new apostle chooses to oppose Peter, one of the original twelve. It was a nerve-wracking experience, but Paul cared enough to confront Peter's hypocrisy. You see, the early church members typically enjoyed a love feast before worship and communion. Since the new converts were both Jews and Gentiles, a problem arose as to what these folks could and couldn't eat. The Jewish converts still wanted to eat only kosher foods (prepared according to Jewish dietary guidelines); the Gentiles didn't care about that. In addition, many of the Gentiles even ate meat that had been sacrificed to foreign idols, realizing that those false gods didn't even exist. Why waste good meat? Yet the Jews would refuse to eat such meat.

The early church leaders solved the problem by setting two tables at the love feast. Typically, Jews ate at the kosher table (which offered no pork or sacrificed meats), while the Gentiles ate at a separate table with no food restrictions. Paul chose to eat with the Gentiles. After his conversion, Paul didn't view meat as being an issue at all. He was saved by grace, after all, free to live with a heart pure toward God, controlled within by the Holy Spirit. When Peter arrived, he began eating at the Jewish table; however, he slowly changed his mind and started taking some food from the Gentile table.

The problem was that Peter became a bit hypocritical when some elders appeared and he quickly abandoned the Gentile table (although he regularly ate non-kosher food). Paul decided to confront him on this issue. What was it teaching everyone about salvation by grace? Paul's positive confrontation stopped a theological drift in the early church. He saw that this hypocrisy would split the church in half if it continued. Instead, he cared enough to confront Peter, envisioning an impending tidal wave of wrong behavior. He stopped it before it grew out of control and required a "blowup" to change it.

Parents who TRUST enough to confront learn from Paul that confrontation does not have to wait until conflict is so heated that it causes relational blowup. Paul saw a small symptom of a larger problem (church division based upon legalism), and he acted. We parents can learn from Paul that as we listen and know our children, we will see small symptoms that might become larger problems. If we care enough to confront, we have the ability to stop the smaller problem before it grows and destroys the child, the relationship, or the family.

Nathan Confronts David

*1 The LORD sent Nathan to David. When he came to him,
he said, "There were two men in a certain town, one rich
and the other poor.
2 The rich man had a very large number of sheep and cattle,
3 but the poor man had nothing except one little ewe lamb
he had bought. He raised it, and it grew up with him and
his children. It shared his food, drank from his cup and
even slept in his arms. It was like a daughter to him.
4 "Now a traveler came to the rich man, but the rich man
refrained from taking one of his own sheep or cattle to prepare a meal for the traveler who had come to him. Instead,
he took the ewe lamb that belonged to the poor man and
prepared it for the one who had come to him."
5 David burned with anger against the man and said to
Nathan, "As surely as the LORD lives, the man who did this
deserves to die!
6 He must pay for that lamb four times over, because he
did such a thing and had no pity."
7 Then Nathan said to David, "You are the man!"*
—2 Samuel 12:1-7 (NIV)

This portion of Scripture sits right in the middle of the account
of David's sin with Bathsheba. In the midst of that sin, God sends
Nathan to speak four words of stinging reproof: "You are the man."
Chuck Swindoll, in his biography of David, writes,

*Whew! Talk about the consequences of sin. David sits there
with his mouth still open leaning back, perhaps staring at
the ceiling, listening to the voice of God from Nathan. Once
silence fills the room, the king drops to his knees as he looks
up into Nathan's clear eyes and says the one thing that is
appropriate, "I have sinned against the Lord."[1]*

Many scholars believe that twelve months had already passed
since the sin of David with Bathsheba. When Nathan entered the

scene, Bathsheba was already pregnant, and Uriah her husband was already dead. David had plenty of time to think about what he had done.

Note that Nathan used a parable. It was a simple enough tale, rooted in customs that David understood. Yet the story had great impact as the prophet used airtight logic to force David to make a decision. Nathan had apparently thought out what he wanted to say and then delivered it to David, knowing in advance what David's logical answer would be.

David repents of his sin in verse 13. Nathan confronts him again, this time showing him how God will limit the punishment. Yes, David will have some trouble, but he isn't going to die. The King James Version says, "The Lord hath put away thy sin."

Parents can learn much from Nathan. First, notice that he was willing to confront the king. So often parents, perceiving their kids as being in control, do not take a face-to-face stand with them. Nathan was aware of David's rank, but he saw sin and confronted it. He didn't let David's rank or the circumstances control his attitude in the situation. Nathan didn't let FEAR overcome what needed to be done.

Second, Nathan was thoroughly prepared. He composed a parable instead of barging into David's house and just yelling at him. He thought through what he wanted to communicate and presented it in such a way that David was forced to think and respond to the story, not directly to an accusation. We live in a world that appreciates parables and metaphors. Where other generations liked lists and points (remember Martin Luther's ninety-five theses, the first ninety-five-point sermon). This generation is best taught, according to many, through stories. Parents should take full advantage of the power of metaphors and parables.

Third, although David paid dearly for his sin, Nathan took the time to reassure him. David was not going to die; God had put away his sin. He loved David, cared enough to confront, and cared enough to be passionate. But Nathan was still a counselor and friend.

Paul Confronts Agrippa

In Acts 25:23–26:32, Paul the Apostle is defending himself before King Agrippa. In his testimony, Paul confronts the king in such a way that the king understands Paul and, if we read between the lines, the king may even want to free him. Paul is dynamic and provides a great argument, but he also shows characteristics of caring enough to confront his captor.

In 26:2-11, Paul testifies to being a changed man, unafraid to confess that he once tried to kill Jews. His focus is now on the Resurrection, but his heart is fully open, showing that he too had doubts. He understands his audience and he testifies, staying focused upon the desired outcome.

In verses 12-18, Paul tells of his encounter with Christ. He was in a huge hurry (traveling at midday, in the heat of the desert, shows he was anxious to persecute Christians) to settle the Christian issue. Christ confronts him, and this encounter changes Paul from being an apostle for the Sanhedrin to being an apostle for Christ. Paul uses a familiar phrase to describe his behavior. "Kicking against the goads" refers to a means of training oxen to stop kicking the wagon. Goads were sharp spikes attached to the wagon to hurt the animal when it tried to kick. They were used to teach submission, but Paul employs the phrase to describe himself. Lastly, Paul communicates that he hadn't strayed from his vision. He had called people to repent. He told of this mission, and the king was impressed.

We can learn from Paul's confrontation, as well. First, Paul accepted the challenge to confront the king. Instead of just accepting the fact that he was going to Rome with his life on the line, he took a shot at communicating the Gospel message to another unsaved person. Many times parents accept the current reality rather than confronting their children and helping them see how things could be different. They do not care enough to confront and train; rather, they accept and let a child continue with wrong behavior.

Second, Paul's heart was open. He wasn't afraid to tell the king that he, too, had sinned. Many times parents are afraid to be open and honest with their children. They may have the same fears or concerns as their children, but they hide them. They don't care enough to confront openly and honestly, letting down their guard and being vulnerable enough to reveal their own feelings.

Further, Paul was an opportunist. He took advantage of his circumstances to defend himself and present the Gospel message. Parents need to be opportunists as well, caring enough to confront when situations present themselves. Many times parents wait until the right moment . . . and the right moment never comes.

Jesus Confronts the Pharisees

6 On another Sabbath he went into the synagogue and was teaching, and a man was there whose right hand was shriveled.
7 The Pharisees and the teachers of the law were looking for a reason to accuse Jesus, so they watched him closely to see if he would heal on the Sabbath.
8 But Jesus knew what they were thinking and said to the man with the shriveled hand, "Get up and stand in front of everyone." So he got up and stood there.
9 Then Jesus said to them, "I ask you, which is lawful on the Sabbath: to do good or to do evil, to save life or to destroy it?"
10 He looked around at them all, and then said to the man, "Stretch out your hand." He did so, and his hand was completely restored.
11 But they were furious and began to discuss with one another what they might do to Jesus.
—Luke 6:6-11 (NIV)

Jesus is confronting the Pharisees over the law, but He is also demonstrating to us what can happen if we don't care enough to confront. The religious leaders saw problems; Jesus saw need. The religious leaders chose to confront in a destructive way, trying to find fault with Jesus and His ministry; Jesus chose to confront short-sightedness and legalism. The religious leaders chose not to confront directly, and their scheming demonstrates the path parents could take if they are fearful. When we choose not to confront—or confront in unhealthy ways—it leads to a critical spirit. And a critical spirit can lead to three damaging patterns:

•*It leads to suspicion.* A critical spirit engenders suspicion. In Luke 6:2, we see another confrontation over the Law. Jesus and His disciples were walking along one of the paths that intersected some grainfields. The fact that the disciples picked and ate some of the grain was in itself no crime. One of the better laws of the Old Testament stated that anyone passing through a field was free to pluck the grain so long as he didn't put a sickle into it (see Deut. 23:25). On any other day, there would have been no complaint; but this was the Sabbath. Four of the forbidden kinds of work were reaping, threshing, winnowing, and preparing food, so technically the disciples had broken every one of them. By plucking the grain, they were guilty of reaping. By rubbing it in their hands, of threshing. By flinging away the husks, of winnowing. And the fact that they ate showed they'd prepared food on the Sabbath. To us, the whole thing seems fantastic, but we must remember that to a strict Pharisee this was deadly sin. Rules and regulations had been broken; here was a matter of life and death.

Nevertheless, their question springs from a spirit of suspicion. Instead of confronting Jesus on one of several other issues, they chose to question His motives, seeking to trap him. No concern for dialogue from this crowd! They only saw problems, and they were allowing FEAR (Future Events Appearing Real) to control their confrontation.

Parents can easily develop a suspicious nature when they don't confront their children in the right ways. When doubt lingers without confrontation, the matter festers like an unhealed sore. Suspicions creep in, and adults begin to make assumptions about certain behaviors. Suspicion leads to FEAR and destructive relationships with children. It's a an easy cycle to enter, but difficult to escape.

•*It leads to accusation.* Luke 6:7 reads, "The scribes and the Pharisees watched him to see whether he would cure on the Sabbath, so that they might find an accusation against him" (NRSV). They weren't looking for constructive ways to confront (like Nathan in the previous example). Rather, they were looking for ways to accuse Jesus. Parents can fall into this same trap as they look for ways to accuse their children. It is far better to confront positively than to sit back and develop accusations.

Accusations also don't give a person credit for how she has changed her life. We parents sometimes fail to rejoice in how far our children have come. We've been blinded by the one little thing that is still "wrong" or missing at this moment, instead of praising all the positive developments. An accusatory mindset focuses attention upon small acts while ignoring the bigger picture of growth and learning in the child.

•*It leads to retaliation.* Luke 6:11 says, "They were furious and began to discuss with one another what they might do to Jesus" (NIV). When parents don't confront their children the right way, or soon enough, two things happen. First, parents get angry. Just like the John Wayne movie where Duke has to come into town, finally pushed to the limit, and clean out the bad guys, so parents get angry and blow up. Caring confrontation doesn't allow the pot of anger to simmer. It releases the pressure that's building and allows both the parents and children to air their feelings and calm down.

Second, failure to contront fosters more plotting and scheming. Too often parents scheme against their children's behaviors instead of learning to confront and work things out. Look at these Pharisees; they saw problems instead of needs. Do you think they, for a moment, tried to understand Jesus and His mission? Apparently not. They had their own turf to protect.

Let's take time to understand our children's needs and temperaments. Let's begin listening a little more closely. That way, we won't fall into a pattern of scheming but rather we'll enter into constructive conversation. Even agreeing to disagree is healthier than plotting and scheming, right?

WILL YOU CONFRONT EFFECTIVELY?

We have a natural "fight or flight" response built into us. When faced with conflict, most of us will either stay and fight or run away. Depending on our temperament, we may push too hard with our fangs bared, or we may just turn and scamper away from any potentially emotional situation. Both extremes are dangerous if we care enough and TRUST enough to confront. Parents who care will learn to move away from the extreme manifestations of their temperaments and manage to confront their children boldly and calmly when necessary. The Book of 2 Samuel provides a negative example of what happens when we choose not to confront.

In 2 Samuel 13–15 we read a story of poor communication and lack of confrontation in David's family. Absalom had heard that his half brother Amnon had raped his sister Tamar, yet he failed to confront Amnon. This was mistake number one. Instead of confronting Amnon, Absalom arranges for Amnon's murder. After Amnon is dead, Absalom flees.

King David has his own part in this soap-opera-like story. David also fails to confront Amnon. After Amnon's death, David increases his problems by not properly settling his conflict with Absalom.

13 The woman said, "Why then have you devised a thing like this against the people of God? When the king says this, does he not convict himself, for the king has not brought back his banished son?
14 Like water spilled on the ground, which cannot be recovered, so we must die. But God does not take away life; instead, he devises ways so that a banished person may not remain estranged from him.
—2 Samuel 14:13-14 (NIV)

Joab knew that David's heart longed for his son, so he has a woman disguise herself and confront the king. Joab, like Nathan, wasn't afraid to confront with the truth. David believes the woman's story about a troubled family, and the woman craftily turns the tables on David, revealing his own guilt within his family. David relents, but Absalom spends three years displaced from his father. David then waits another two years before he actually sees his son. What makes matters worse, David was so afraid of confronting his son that his son had to finally force the meeting. This isn't exactly a great example of positive confrontation.

"Absalom behaved in this way toward all the Israelites who came to the king asking for justice, and so he stole the hearts of the men of Israel" (2 Sam. 15:6, NIV). Absalom was so angry at his father that he plotted to take away the hearts of the people along with his father's kingdom. David's failure to confront brought him and his kingdom into intense conflict. Had David chosen to deal with the issues—cared enough to confront his son—Amnon's murder and Absalom's conspiracy could have been avoided.

Parents in similar situations can learn from David. Instead of fleeing conflict due to fear, they need to take prompt action. Dealing directly with disagreements is so much better than simply ignoring them. David shows the strain that can arise in relationships when problems fester apart from quick and caring confrontation. Did David need to bull his way into the situation? No, he just needed to practice effective confrontation.

It's clear that some people, even from ancient times, try to avoid their family problems at all costs. That doesn't work! Yet there is correct and effective confrontation and there is improper and ineffective confrontation. Do you know the difference?

Of course, proper confrontation does not always achieve the results we're after. That depends heavily on others' responses, which may be evil, for instance. Nevertheless, we do need to know the difference between good and bad methods of confrontation. Many models of proper confrontation exist in the Scriptures. Matthew 18 offers one of the best:

> *15 If your brother sins against you, go and show him his fault, just between the two of you. If he listens to you, you have won your brother over.*
> *16 But if he will not listen, take one or two others along, so that "every matter may be established by the testimony of two or three witnesses."*
> *17 If he refuses to listen to them, tell it to the church; and if he refuses to listen even to the church, treat him as you would a pagan or a tax collector.*
> —Matthew 18:15-17 (NIV)

•*Tackle the concern head-on.* Notice that Jesus' words don't suggest timidity, but rather action. The original-language word for "sin" implies "missing the mark," so when parents are uncomfortable with behavior, or see something that needs to be discussed, it is usually something that misses the mark. Tackle head-on whatever misses the mark. We must never tolerate any situation in which there is a breach of personal relationships between us and another member of our family. Recognize the issue and move to the next step.

•*Go directly to the child.* I know of a mother who spends time on the telephone gossiping about her children. Obviously, when the kids are home, they hear what their mother is saying.

Essentially, this mom is afraid to confront her children directly, so she talks to friends on the telephone about the problems. Scripture commands us to go directly to the person with whom we have conflict. This means a face-to-face meeting. Priority number one on Jesus' list seemed to be such a meeting. The word used in the original text means "alone without a companion." No sense getting the neighbors involved when the disagreement or concern can be solved face-to-face.

•*Go to the child quickly.* Matthew 5:24 tells us to "leave your gift there in front of the altar. First go and be reconciled to your brother; then come and offer your gift" (NIV). The appropriate response, before anything else, is to go to the offending person. This may mean we swallow our pride, but Jesus doesn't care about pride, He cares about relationships. No matter who is at fault, it's the parents' responsibility to go quickly and resolve the conflict through timely confrontation. Parents can't expect to have a right relationship with God if relational issues are seething among family members. Scripture calls us to go quickly and face our conflicts.

If we don't go quickly it becomes easy for the enemy to lead is to FEAR instead of TRUST. We must TRUST God for that first step and realize that if we hang back, in FEAR, we will leave open the gates of a critical spirit and vain imaginings. Far better for us to eat some humble pie than allow those two relationship-destroying attitudes to get in the way.

•*Bring in the reserves.* In Matthew 18 Jesus outlines some effective steps to conflict resolution through direct and quick confrontation. He shows us when to bring in the reserves. I'm not recommending the old, "wait until your father/mother gets home" approach; it's best to go directly to the child. However, if that isn't working, ask the other parent or someone else to join the conversation.

Though ganging up doesn't work, sometimes other people can help the parent fully understand what is being said. Often we get so involved in the conversation (or argument) that we lose our good listening skills. The other person can take a neutral stance and help each side hear the other more clearly.

•*Create the right environment.* Effective parents create an environment that encourages discussion and the freedom to speak and be heard. The right environment includes:

—*Patience.* This must be applied to the process of confrontation and the person involved. We do well to proceed with patience, in spite of our frustrations, the child's apparent failings, and all the inconveniences created. We'll likely need to set aside our agenda for a while, our push to get something done. Only with patience do we clear away obstacles and resistance.

—*Gentleness.* This is a spirit of tenderness instead of harshness, hardness, or forcefulness. Remember, we're attempting to open up an atmosphere in our home that fosters sharing, transparency, and vulnerability. All of this must be wrapped in a predictable gentleness. Children need to feel they are being listened to and that any feeling is OK to reveal with appropriate self-reporting. (Of course, not every feeling is appropriate to act upon without boundaries!) A spirit of gentleness can quickly help parents over emotional hurdles and on to reconciliation or problem solving.

—*Acceptance.* This means withholding judgment, giving the benefit of the doubt, and requiring no evidence or specific performance as a condition for sustaining love. Acceptance opens up the child as you, for that moment, make him or her your number-one priority.

—*Kindness.* Kindness is sensitive, caring, and thoughtful. It is remembering the little things (which are the big things) in relationships.

—*Openness.* Essential to quality confrontation is the ability to acquire accurate information and perspectives about your children and the issues at hand. It means giving full consideration to their intentions, desires, values, and goals rather than focusing exclusively on their behaviors.

—*Temperament.* Remember to keep your children's temperaments in mind. Are you confronting little Johnny in a style that is likely to "speak" to him, in particular? Or, are you bulling ahead without regard to how God made him? Are you checking for backup styles and avoiding moving into a disruptive backup style tension?

—*Listening.* Always remember to listen. Seek to understand what children are saying before trying to rebut or argue. Read the body language. Listen below the surface. Confrontational time is their time as well; it isn't just a use of your own precious time. Therefore, take time to listen completely and work hard to make the meeting of minds valuable for everyone.

—*Unity*. Ephesians 4:3 says, "Make every effort to keep the unity of the Spirit through the bond of peace" (NIV). One of parents' goals in confrontation should be to maintain unity with children. Unity is a powerful tool in families, an especially powerful witness to the neighbors.

—*Peace*. The preferred outcome is the bond of peace. I have seen many households destroyed because there wasn't a common striving for peace. This doesn't mean we avoid confrontation. Far from it! It means that parents work hard with their children always with the goal of peace in mind. The purpose of confrontation is to reach the shore of peace, but there may be much rough water to cross along the way. Never go to bed angry with your children. Settle the dispute before the sun sets on the day—an unsettled dispute can only lead to suspicion and vain imaginings, plus hurt feelings.

—*Humility*. Ephesians 4:2 reminds us to be completely humble. This is so important during confrontation with children. If parents react with a spirit of brassy confidence, if they go into the confrontation thinking they know it all, then they will miss the point and disappoint the child. Scripture calls us to be humble.

—*Love*. Always approach confrontation out of a spirit of love. Scripture says to "bear each other up in love." If parents are angry when they go into confrontation, they will not be able to focus on listening, humility, unity, etc. They will simply want to make a point, in anger, and thus be defeated by the enemy.

—*Consistency*. This requires a clear set of values, a personal code. Consistency flows from a manifestation of your character and a reflection of who you are and who you are becoming. Consistency helps the child to see you as a solid, dependable person instead of one who is tossed by the wind and waves.

—*Integrity*. Integrity matches words to actions. Here there is no desire to deceive, take advantage of, manipulate, or control. It is constantly reviewing your intentions as you strive for balance in your relationships with your children.

—*Compassionate confrontation*. With this you can help children to make "mid-course corrections" in a context of genuine care,

concern, and warmth. Such compassion makes it safe for children
to risk mistakes and errors. These are learning experiences too!
Positive risk is better than fear of failure.[2]

Ultimately, confrontation will lead parents to better relationships
with their children. Isn't that what we all want? As we work together, we grow together, making positive adjustments as we continue
to learn about each other's needs. Each time Pam and I confronted
our children it was difficult and risky. But I can honestly say those
times caused our relationships to strengthen and grow. They were
worth every minute of time, every tear shed, every question raised.

THINK AND TALK ABOUT IT

1. How does positive confrontation teach discernment to children?
2. How do you plan to confront troubling behavior the next time
   you see it in your family?
3. What are some ways to confront compassionately?
4. What are some typical approaches people adopt in conflicts or
   disagreements?
5. What steps did Jesus set forth about confrontation?

Notes

1 Charles R. Swindoll, *David: A Man of Passion and Destiny*, 203.

2 Some of these keys are adapted from Stephen R. Covey, *Principle-Centered
Leadership* (New York: Summit Books, 1990), 107-108.

Chapter 10

TRUSTING ENOUGH TO DISCIPLINE

THE MAN INVITED HIS FRIEND OVER for tea in his beautiful rose garden. He'd taken great pains over the years to carefully plan and cultivate this garden, and he enjoyed inviting people over to share tea and conversation among the gorgeous flowers. On this particular day, the visitor began talking about his children. He told his host that he and his wife had decided to stop disciplining their children. After all, the children needed to be free to enjoy life and not be burdened by punishment and correction.

The host simply nodded, choosing not to debate his good friend.

Some months later the gardener invited his friend back for tea and conversation. When the guest arrived, he noticed that the beautiful rose garden was a shambles. It was full of ugly weeds, the roses wildly growing in every direction, and the weeds overtaking everything. When the host appeared to serve the tea, his guest exclaimed, "What has happened to your beautiful garden!"

The host replied, "Oh, that. Well, I decided after you left the last time to apply your sense of discipline to my garden. After all, why should my plants not be free, like your children, to simply enjoy themselves?"

The answer, of course, was that *true beauty must be cultivated.* And cultivation is the essence of discipline. It's the cultivation of right thinking, of sterling character, of praiseworthy actions that will blossom into a lifetime of integrity. Who of us wouldn't want this kind of beauty for our children?

The entire process begins with the radical obedience. I can hear parents lifting resounding cheers: "Yes, yes! This is what we need! Bring it on!" Unfortunately, at this point, I'm not talking about the obedience of children. Rather, I speak of the need for radical obedience in parents. (I hear the air going out of the balloon, but please bear with me for a few more sentences!) You see, some parents' favorite saying is, "Do as I say, not as I do." That never made sense to me and still doesn't. The question is, how can parents expect discipline from their children when they are not disciplined themselves? Isn't that a bit hypocritical? Joyce Meyer writes, "Without discipline and self-control, there can be no permanent victory in our lives. Dreams and visions won't come true unless we hear from God and discipline ourselves to follow His guidance and leadership."[1] Hebrews 10:5-7 says,

When Christ came into the world, he said: "Sacrifice and offering you did not desire, but a body you prepared for me; with burnt offerings and sin offerings you were not pleased. Then I said, 'Here I am—it is written about me in the scroll—I have come to do your will, O God'" (NIV).

The Lord Jesus developed as a leader through personal discipline, through reverent submission, and through pain and opposition. His attitude of radical obedience to God was crucial to his development. We are to follow Christ's example and literally "come to do the Father's will"—what He wishes us to do. Christ came for many reasons, but the foundation of all He did was centered on doing the will of His father. That is radical obedience.

If you truly love God, then you are truly involved in loving His plans and seeking His guidance with each decision that comes your way. Now, think of your parenting role. Is what you do as a parent totally and completely involved with God? If not, imagine being able to say "I am here as a parent to completely do God's will. I'm submitting myself in radical obedience to God, His plan for my life, and the plan He has for my children." Parents who make this statement—parents who are growing and developing in their faith—can effectively discipline their children. Why? Because if you truly desire to be radically obedient to God's plan, then you will model, daily, the behavior you expect from your children.

Now, if you haven't come to this place in your life, don't worry. Remember FEAR and TRUST? We are all on a journey away from FEAR and toward TRUST. Radical obedience comes a day, an hour, and a minute at a time. I once had a very bad temper. When I became a Christian, I knew I needed God's help to get this temper under control. It didn't happen overnight. It took much prayer, support from my wife, and study of Scripture to help me control my raging and radically obey God in this area of my life. If God was willing to help me, I know He will help any parent who honestly wants His help. TRUST Him today, right now; be radically obedient to Him. Then you'll be prepared to cultivate your children into the most beautiful adults.

WHAT, EXACTLY, IS DISCIPLINE?

For the purpose of this study, let's assume that the goal of discipline is to make disciples out of our children. The word "discipline" comes from a Latin word *disco* (no, not the dance), which means "to learn or get to know," implying a direct acquaintance with something or someone. Discipline, then, refers to the process by which one learns a way of life.[2]

That is exactly what parental discipline is meant to achieve. Parents use discipline to help their children learn and cultivate a way of life. Negative discipline leads to negative children, while positive discipline leads children to a positive lifestyle. Yelling, scolding, and name-calling produce children who have low self-esteem, anger (either expressed or repressed), and shame. Counseling, teaching, and being a positive role model leads to children with good self-images, positive outlooks, and personalities that are shame-free. So let's look a little closer at how this kind of discipline works. Here are nine of its primary qualities:

Discipline Focuses on Instruction

Discipline is instruction. Just like the gardener in the opening illustration, we need to cultivate in our children the behavior that will develop beauty of character and joy in following the Lord. We have a large rose tree in our backyard. We don't want it growing up the side of the house, but we do want it to grow within the trellis structure. We need to train it, instruct it to do what is best for it and us.

Proverbs 3:11 tells our children, "Do not despise the Lord's discipline and do not resent his rebuke, because the LORD disciplines those he loves, as a father the son he delights in" (NIV). The word "discipline" implies correction and rebuke. How can parents correct and rebuke without conveying instruction at the same time?

Note that "discipline" in verse 11 translates the Hebrew word *muwcar*. It refers to teaching one how to live correctly in the fear of the Lord, so that he learns his lesson before temptation and testing come. What better way to instruct children than *before* they encounter temptation and testing? Discipline doesn't need to be an after-the-fact punishment, but rather an instruction in preparation for any trouble ahead.

In this regard, we always had frank discussions in our home about drugs and premarital sex. Pam and I wanted to help our children make decisions about right and wrong before they were put in front of a specific temptation. We laid out all the facts and consequences we could develop. We did it often, and we allowed our kids to ask as many questions as they wished. We were using instruction to discipline—to prepare them for life.

Discipline Offers Guidance

Discipline is a form of guidance. We live in an agricultural area with thousands of acres dedicated to growing grapes; in fact, wine making is one of the largest local industries. I never realized there was such a detailed system for growing grapevines until I looked a little more closely at one of the vineyards. Wires are used to guide the vines into the best shape for producing fruit. The vines are disciplined in this sense for the best results.

Our first house had nine fruit trees growing in the backyard. The people who had previously owned the house had planted the trees but let them grow wild. The branches grew in every direction, and the fruit was not good. All except for one apricot tree. Apparently, the previous owners liked apricots and had carefully pruned this tree. It had a great shape and produced much fruit. They had "guided" its growth so it produced a ton of goodness.

God gave us the Ten Commandments for similar reasons. Many people look at these words of wisdom as barriers to fun and freedom. They feel inhibited by the restrictive "do's" and "don'ts." But do they not serve our own best interests? Years ago we attended a Christian camp where Luis Palau was speaking, and his topic was the Ten Commandments. For five days, Palau showed us how the commandments were not God-given barriers to our growth, but freeing boundaries to a Spirit-filled life. For example, Exodus 20:14 says, "You shall not commit adultery." Palau pointed out that I'm so much more free to love my wife, and my wife is free to love me, when our love stays within the boundary of marriage. I can love her as much as I want—avoiding all kinds of grievous complications and heartaches—as long as I don't jump over the fence to adultery. I am protected and nurtured by that fence.

This is an example of the loving guidance of effective discipline. Disney World uses ropes and poles to gently guide guests in line and onto rides. Guide dogs help people who have difficulty seeing; tour guides take uninstructed tourists to locations they have never seen; and guidance counselors help students assemble a curriculum so they can reach an educational goal. Guidance is a necessary form of discipline.

Discipline Sometimes Punishes

We don't like this one, but it too is an essential part of discipline. Remember David and Bathsheba? David sinned, was confronted by Nathan, and repented. However, David's sin had terrible consequences, including the death of an infant. Every day on the news we see a whole society of folks who want to be free of consequences for personal wrongdoing. People blame their misconduct on all kinds of outside circumstances, and they run from the consequences. We are fast becoming a discipline-free society.

Psalm 94:12-13 says, "Blessed is the man you discipline, O LORD, the man you teach from your law; you grant him relief from days of trouble, till a pit is dug for the wicked" (NIV). *The Life Application Bible* notes for this verse say, "At times, God must discipline us to help us. This is similar to a loving parent's disciplining his child. The discipline isn't very enjoyable to the child, but it's essential to teach him right from wrong. The Bible says that 'no discipline seems pleasant at the time, but painful. Later on, however, it produces a harvest of righteousness and peace for those who have been trained by it'" (Heb. 12:11, NIV).[3]

The punishment involved in discipline can be applied in many ways. It can mean restrictions, time out, extra work, or, in some cases, spanking. In his book *Becoming the Parent God Wants You to Be*, Kevin Leman addresses this issue:

> *Can "pulling the rug out" and letting children experience the consequences ever include spanking? Yes, I believe there are times a spanking is an appropriate response, but it should rarely be the first response.*[4]

He goes on to give some practical ideas for spanking:

- *A spanking may be in order as all other "reality discipline" fails.*
- *Most appropriate for children in the two-to-seven age range.*
- *Spanking is two or three swats to the bottom followed by holding the child and assuring him or her of your love.*
- *Use your hand so you know how much pain is inflicted.*
- *Always spank in private.*
- *Never spank when you are angry.*
- *Watch the frequency of spanking. If it is becoming an everyday thing, check on acceptance, love, and encouragement for the child.*[5]

Discipline Attempts to Be Constructive

Discipline should always be a path to child development. It needs to help the child realize wrong behavior and then offer an opportunity to change that behavior. Discipline isn't something that simply tears down a child and leaves him or her stranded on the road to growth as a human being.

When Jennifer was in middle school, she wanted us to buy her some very expensive pants. We didn't have the budget for such an extravagant expense, especially just to wear to school. She, however, needed to feel part of the group and desperately wanted those pants. Her normally cheerful attitude plummeted, and her disappointment was reflected in how she began to treat us.

We decided to discipline her for her rather selfish attitudes. We told her what we would be willing to pay for a regular pair of pants for school. We decided that since she wanted these pants so badly that she could purchase them if she raised the difference in what we were allowing (what our budget said we could spend) and the actual price of the pants.

She worked for weeks for neighbors and friends doing mostly babysitting and odd jobs. When she'd saved enough money, she asked if she could go to the store. To our surprise, when she got there, she decided not to buy the pants. She realized that she could purchase two pairs of regular pants and even have some money left over!

This constructive discipline (not caving in to her whim of wanting "the" pair of pants) helped her to begin understanding the value of money, the value of saving, and the value of work. She walked away from the store much happier, and we were able to help her find "the right way" through constructive discipline.

Discipline Remains Consistent

Staying consistent is like constructing a toy castle out of building blocks. We make a decision, and then place another on top of that, then another, as each decision becomes a block in a very large wall. When we put in a block that is a strange size (inconsistent with the rest) the wall becomes shaky and may even crack or collapse. When the wall begins to weaken, it is vulnerable to hypocrisy and lack of integrity; it confuses those who rely upon it for unwavering strength and wisdom. John 7:22-23 (NASB) gives us a great example of inconsistency.

> On this account Moses has given you circumcision (not because it's from Moses, but from the fathers), and on the Sabbath you circumcise a man. If a man receives circumcision on the Sabbath that the Law of Moses may not be broken, are you angry with Me because I made an entire man well on the Sabbath?

In His teaching, Jesus was always pointing out the inconsistency of the laws and grace. In this case, the Jewish leaders could circumcise on the Sabbath, but they criticized Jesus for healing on the Sabbath. They were not consistent.

Some basics on being consistent:

• Firmly establish the rules. Help children completely understand the rules, so they clearly know what is right and wrong. Kids need to know what is expected of them.

• Discipline in private so the child isn't humiliated in front of others.

• Clearly explain why you are discipling the child. Let him or her know what went wrong, where he or she broke the rule or behavioral expectations.

• Continue to love the child unconditionally, as always, no matter what the wrongdoing, its consequences, or its punishment.

One night little Zachary broke one of our house rules, a rule that carried with it a maximum sentence—a spanking. I don't remember his particular infraction, but I do remember those brown eyes looking up at me, and before I could swat his behind, the tears flowed from both our eyes. I held him in my arms, we prayed together, and I told him how much I loved him. He understood we had to be consistent, and today I can look very proudly at a son who understands the value of consistency and integrity.

Discipline Proceeds with Balance

Discipline doesn't work if it isn't balanced. Not every act is a reason to inflict the expected punishment. It becomes routine if parents administer discipline without some creativity, flexibility, and mercy. With each event we must consider the circumstances: what are the mitigating factors in terms of the child's motives, intentions, understandings? What is her attitude after the event? Is she contrite? belligerent? brokenhearted? Carefully weigh all of these factors before meting out some form of punishment. Or perhaps the natural consequences of an ill-advised action are punishment enough. Sometimes a teen may simply need a clear and direct statement of your disapproval or disappointment.

In any case, screaming at children makes no sense. We were at the store the other day observing a mother in the checkout line. While she was paying for her groceries, her son, about four years old, became intrigued with the little impulse stuff displayed at the counter. She was ready to go, but little Ben wasn't. So she yelled at him (really, more of a whine), "Let's go, Beeeeen!" He chose not to move. Mother had whined so many times in the past without any consequence, so why should this time be any different? He just stayed and played in the stuff, now holding up the line.

Ben's mother was diligent, and the next step in the process (or the "game," if you are Ben) was for her to say, "OK, Ben, I'm going to count; this is *one*!" Ben remained where he was. "OK, Beeeeen, this is *two*." Ben was unwavering; he just kept playing, and now the grocery line was quite long. Finally, with great flair, the mother walked over to Ben, picked him up by the shoulders and proceeded to carry him out of the store. No number three, no discipline, just "Oh well, nothing else works, so I'll save myself some embarrassment and just tote him out on my hip."

Obviously, Ben's mother was out of balance, and so was Ben. She had many times before tried yelling and whining. She had done the counting game and never followed through. Therefore, in frustration, she just carried him away. But suppose she'd walked over to him, looked him straight in the eye, and said, "Ben, it's over. We are leaving, and you are coming with me"? Then, in private, she could have explained to Ben what he had done wrong and followed though with appropriate punishment.

Discipline Creates Wise Choices

As parents develop their children through discipline, the process should ultimately lead to helping children learn to make their own wise choices. I talked earlier about Jennifer and her desire to purchase some expensive pants. It was our heartfelt desire to show her how to make wise choices in such situations. Good decision-making is a skill our children will need throughout their lives. One goal of discipline must be, therefore, to help them develop in this area.

Proverbs 19:20 says, "Get all the advice you can and be wise the rest of your life" (TLB). Children need to see us as their counselors or advisors. As they experience our consistency, love, instruction, guidance, and correction, they will naturally come to us for counsel.

When Esau was forty years old, he married Judith daughter of Beeri the Hittite, and also Basemath daughter of Elon

the Hittite. They were a source of grief to Isaac and Rebekah.
—Genesis 26:34-35 (NIV)

Esau married pagan women, and this deeply upset his parents. Yet they apparently hadn't taken the time to discipline him and help him make wise choices. This kind of upset can usually be avoided if parents invest significant time in the right kind of discipline, with the goal of developing the child's own decision-making tools.

Discipline Demonstrates Caring

I firmly believe that discipline, done correctly, shows kids that parents care. More often than not, children left to their own devices come to realize that their parents don't care enough to even give them clear-cut boundaries. Misbehavior continues as a child seeks this indicator of parental attention and love.

5 And you have forgotten that word of encouragement that addresses you as sons: "My son, do not make light of the Lord's discipline, and do not lose heart when he rebukes you,
6 because the Lord disciplines those he loves, and he punishes everyone he accepts as a son."
7 Endure hardship as discipline; God is treating you as sons. For what son is not disciplined by his father?
8 If you are not disciplined (and everyone undergoes discipline), then you are illegitimate children and not true sons.
9 Moreover, we have all had human fathers who disciplined us and we respected them for it. How much more should we submit to the Father of our spirits and live!
10 Our fathers disciplined us for a little while as they thought best; but God disciplines us for our good, that we may share in his holiness.
11 No discipline seems pleasant at the time, but painful. Later on, however, it produces a harvest of righteousness and peace for those who have been trained by it.
—Hebrews 12:5-11 (NIV)

The ultimate punishment is for God to leave us alone when He realizes we are unteachable and beyond change. What a haunting and lonely thought! Parents who don't discipline (according to the guidelines outlined in this chapter) are producing children who feel abandoned, unloved, and uncared for. They haven't been loved enough to be taught, guided, or disciplined.

Discipline Remains Confidential

Finally, remember to discipline children one-on-one in a private place. I can remember taking one of our children to the men's room during church services, for example. It was important to us that we didn't add embarrassment to the pain of being disciplined. This applies to verbal discipline as well as for spanking: do it in private.

God is a just and faithful God. When He reproves us, he doesn't do it in a crowd. He does it alone, in quiet moments. Nathan approached David in a quiet moment, and Jesus, in Matthew 18, recommended that we go to our offending brother one-on-one. Discipline isn't easy, so why would parents want to add further frustration to their children by making a scene in front of a crowd of strangers—or other family members?

WHAT DISCIPLINE *ISN'T* . . .

This topic is so important that I'd like to approach it from the opposite side for a moment. We've talked about key qualities of discipline, but perhaps detailing what it *isn't* will round out the picture.

Discipline Is NOT the Result of Rage

God's Word doesn't have many positive words for a person with a bad temper. The Old Testament word used for "hot-tempered" literally means "nostrils" or "nose." Perhaps the idea is that a raging person puts his nose "in your face." Don't make friends with someone like that!

24 Do not make friends with a hot-tempered man, do not associate with one easily angered,
25 or you may learn his ways and get yourself ensnared.
—Proverbs 22:24-25 (NIV)

There's simply no place in discipline for inappropriate, raging anger. It defeats the whole process. The child realizes the parent is out of control, and any discipline loses its teaching value when delivered in out-of-control anger.

Parents can learn how to curb this kind of anger—believe me, I know from first-hand experience. They can control their feelings by (1) recognizing their reaction for what it is, (2) praying for strength, and (3) asking God for help to see the opportunities that even the current bad situation can provide. Authors Gary Smalley and John Trent write:

> Often, the first response by parents can set the tone for how traumatically an event will be taken. . . . When one of my children is hurting, compounding it by reacting with angry words doesn't add to the solution. If anything, such a reaction often freezes things in a problem state. Responding with initial softness helps the child see that if Dad and Mom aren't panicking, maybe there is a light at the end of the tunnel. If the child sees his parents panicking or moving into anger, he is often barred from responding in any other way.[6]

Note the dangerous cycle that anger can cause. Parents display a certain reaction, and children mirror it accordingly. If parents choose to "blow up," then chances are that children will grow up angry and ready to blow up too. It seems to be a never-ending cycle that doesn't lead to positive family life or mature adults.

Certainly, bad behavior can cause parents to feel angry. And it is important to let children become familiar with the whole range of human emotion built into them by the Creator. Every child should learn that sometimes people must become angry, show it, and let it move them into constructive action. After all, evil flourishes where there is no righteous indignation. Therefore, we are not attempting to hide our true feelings, since our children can learn from us how to express them appropriately. I'm simply saying that we must *be in control of our rage* as we discipline our children. Otherwise, we'll be thoughtlessly lashing out.

Children have every opportunity to push parents to unbelievable limits. The point is that we shouldn't discipline out of purely reactive anger. Take time to pray, seeking God's response to the situation, and letting the initial white-hot emotion subside before beginning to discipline. An ill-considered angry response can negate much of what we've worked so hard to achieve.

On the other hand, we wouldn't want to teach children that we can hit (spank) with a cool, collected demeanor, a blithe smile adorning our face. No, when we are truly involved with them, their ill behavior fills us with frustration and hurt. It should, and will, come through. Dr. Gary Chapman writes, "The clear challenge of Scripture is that we learn to process anger in a positive, loving manner rather than by explosion or implosion."[7] Clearly the best choice is taking angry feelings to God and allowing Him to put TRUST in our heart for the growth and discipline of our children. If our rage seems to constantly erupt "from out of the blue," we may need to seek counseling and delve into our own childhood experiences in depth. If we've been abused as children, we'll need to spend the required time in grieving our sadness about that and expressing our rage in ways that do not harm our own children. Any insight we gain in this way can only benefit—and perhaps protect!—our kids.

Discipline Is NOT a Form of Abuse

When discipline moves into the arena of abuse, it's outright sin. Abusive behavior by parents is any course of action that leads children to feel shamed. Shame is the dishonor, embarrassment, and humiliation felt by children when parents question their worth as human beings. If guilt is the result of "I *did* something bad," (an appropriate response), then shame is the sense that "I *am* bad" (which is never true). Shaming behavior calls into question the child's essential value rather than her questionable behavior. This can be a subtle distinction, but it has profound effects. Shaming children through any behavior destroys their self-esteem and literally wears them out. Abusive acts by parents lead children down a road of inner pain (and often addiction—the attempt to dull the pain) that can last a lifetime.

Years ago we asked people attending a seminar to respond to a poll. An anonymous questionnaire listed literally hundreds of addictions, abuses, and bad habits. In most cases, over 75 percent of the church-going people who attended our conferences were abused or had an addictive lifestyle (now or in the past). As we began to know the people, it became obvious that many of their problems stemmed from the shaming abuse received from parents.

•*Physical Abuse.* Earlier I mentioned spanking as a possible (if not last-resort) kind of punishment. A quick slap of a child's bottom isn't physical abuse. But beware should that quick slap to the bottom become hard blows to the body! Abuse is also any curtailment of movement such as being tied up, even tickling, if the child is pinned to the floor and not allowed to get free upon request. Physical abuse involves extreme punishment of any kind. We have all read news reports of parents who have held children captive in closets, deprived them of food and/or water, chained them to beds, or beaten them. Once physically abused, children begin to hate and react in rage to any kind of discipline. And they result in adults who are horribly self-abusive and who often live with no regard for authority or society's rules.

•*Emotional and Verbal Abuse.* Emotional and verbal abuse includes aggressive, vicious, degrading, and threatening words. Even certain forms of body language or "the look" can deliver emotional abuse squarely into a child's soul. Constant yelling, nagging, and name-calling also serve to belittle the child and make him or her feel shameful and damaged. Also, stay away from shaming nicknames! How will little "stinky" or "tubby" blossom into a happy well-adjusted adult?

I once had a friend whose father was a Marine drill sergeant. When this father arrived home each day, he couldn't seem to keep his job out of his home life. He treated his children with contempt and strict military discipline. He verbally abused them, called them "sissy," and made fun of their changing pre-teen bodies. Consequently, my friend was an angry and confused boy. With most of the other kids, he was the bully who picked fights and used rather strong language. The family moved away from our neighborhood and I lost track of him, but without the Lord and therapy I can't imagine this boy-now-man being a positive influence in society.

•*Sexual Abuse.* Fondling, ogling, and other behaviors inflicted by parents to arouse or stimulate their children are obviously wrong. Any violation of a child's privacy in a sexual manner can cause a lifetime of emotional dysfunction. It is wrong in the eyes of God and the law, a terrible crime perpetrated on children.

No matter what degree of abuse, the victim always feels shame and overwhelming guilt. If the sexual abuse happened very early on, it may be completely repressed and unavailable to the adult's consciousness. Then the gnawing feelings of guilt and anxiety, the inability to form strong, loving relationships, seems irrational. But it's not; there is a reason; psychological counseling can help. And, of course, parents who are using abuse as a form of punishment or discipline need to seek professional care immediately.

Discipline Is NOT a Waste of Time

Discipline isn't raging reactions, it isn't abuse, and it isn't a waste of a parent's time. It's a positive use of time to cultivate, nurture, instruct, and train children to follow the right path—the path toward Christlike adulthood. "Train up a child in the way he should go: and when he is old, he won't depart from it" (Prov. 22:6). *Adam Clarke's Commentary* on this verse examines the literal translation from the Hebrew here. Clarke writes:

> *"Initiate the child at the opening (the mouth) of his path." When he comes to the opening of the way of life, being able to walk alone, and to choose; stop at this entrance, and begin a series of instructions, how he is to conduct himself in every step he takes. Show him the duties, the dangers, and the blessings of the path; give him directions how to perform the duties, how to escape the dangers, and how to secure the blessings, which all lie before him. Fix these on his mind by daily inculcation, till their impression is become indelible; then lead him to practice by slow and almost imperceptible degrees, till each indelible impression becomes a strongly radiated habit. Beg incessantly the blessing of God on all this teaching and discipline; and then you have obeyed the injunction of the wisest of men.*[8]

The benefit is clear: "he won't depart from it." What great hope for parents! Is discipline a waste of time? Hardly, when the benefit is a child who loves the Lord, studies His Word, and is a positive influence at home and in school. God's promise is that if parents train their children, the children won't depart from that training.

I'm so impressed with the family of Cassie Bernall, a teenager who lost her life in the shootings at Columbine High School. She is the student who, while looking up the barrel of a gun, told the shooter, "Yes, I do believe in God." Cassie's parents have a compelling story to tell. They are strong Christians, yet they were watching their daughter move away from the Lord. Cassie's mother quit her job and both she and her husband decided that prayer and time with Cassie were essential. They were right. Cassie turned her life around and turned to Christ with an eagerness they had never seen. She lost her life to senseless violence; however, God has used her martyrdom to communicate the Gospel to millions of teenagers. After seeing Cassie's parents speaking on a network news program, I can tell that they don't think the time they invested in disciplining Cassie was a waste.

Several years ago, Dr. Thomas P. Johnson, a psychiatrist for the San Diego County Probation Department, wrote these guidelines for parents:

- Don't disapprove of what a child is—disapprove of what he does.
- Give attention and praise for good behavior—not bad behavior.
- Encourage and allow discussion, but remember it is the parents who should make the final decision.
- Punishment should be swift, reasonable, related to the offense, and absolutely certain to occur—but it need not be severe.
- Throw out all the rules you are unwilling to enforce and be willing to change the rules if and when you think they need changing.
- Don't lecture and don't warn—youngsters will remember what they think is important to remember.
- Don't feel you have to justify rules, although you should try to explain them.
- As your youngster grows older, many rules may be subject to discussion and compromise. The few rules you really feel strongly about should be enforced no matter what rules other parents have.
- Allow a child to assume responsibility for his decisions as he shows the ability to do so.

• Don't expect children to demonstrate more self control than you do.

• Be honest with your children—hypocrisy shows.

The most important factor in your child's self-image is what he thinks you think of him. His self-image is a major factor in how he conducts himself.[9]

One final word: children need to see that you, Mom and Dad, are a united front. They shouldn't be able to find an opening where they can play one of you against the other in order to manipulate the situation. Pam never challenged my opinion on discipline in front of the children. She waited until we could be alone. We never debated our decisions in front of the children; we did it in private and then came to our kids united in purpose and method. Parents are a team, not two individuals, when it comes to discipline.

Parents who apply TRUST toward discipline see it as a way to positively shape and care for what God has so richly blessed them with. Discipline is nothing more than training, coaching, and helping children to become all that God wants them to be.

THINK AND TALK ABOUT IT

1. What is the purpose and goal of discipline?
2. What do we learn about God from the fact that He disciplines us?
3. How might you change your discipline strategies based on what you've read in this chapter?

Notes

1 Joyce Meyer, "From Frustration to Victory," *Life in the Word*, Vol. 13, No. 9.

2 *Holman Bible Dictionary*, (Holman Bible Publishers, 1991. Used by special arrangement with Broadman & Holman Publishers. Database: NavPress Software.)

3 *New Testament Life Application Notes and Bible Helps* © 1986 owned by assignment by Tyndale House Publishers, Inc., Harmony of the Gospels © 1986 by James C. Galvin. All rights reserved. Used by permission.

4 Kevin Leman, *Becoming the Parent God Wants You to Be*, 189.

5 Ibid., 189. "Reality Discipline" is a phrase coined by Dr. Leman. Reality discipline is

training your child with the combined power of love and limits.

6 *Men's Devotional Bible* (Grand Rapids, MI: Zondervan Publishing House, 1993), 1211.

7 Gary Chapman, *The Other Side of Love* (Chicago: Moody Press, 1999), 85.

8 *Adam Clarke's Commentary*, Electronic text and markup © 1999 by Epiphany Software.

9 Beverly LaHaye, *How to Develop Your Child's Temperament*, 148.

Chapter 11

TRUSTING ENOUGH FOR PRAYERFUL INVOLVEMENT

HAVE YOU READ TOM BROKAW'S BOOK *The Greatest Generation?* What a testimony to the men and women who lived and served during World War II! Brokaw firmly believes this is the greatest generation in America's history. He tells story after story of these wonderful people and how they assumed their difficult responsibilities without complaint. They had a passionate determination to save America and her allies from oppression. They worked hard, soldiered hard, and came home to convert a wartime economy into one of the greatest peacetime economic booms ever seen in the history of the world. Brokaw writes, "I am in awe of them, and I feel privileged to have been a witness to their lives and their sacrifices."[1]

Yes, these ordinary people knew what it meant to take responsibility. They didn't make excuses, didn't whine or blame the other fellow. This generation took what was dealt to them and made the very best of it. What a fitting description of parents who TRUST enough to get involved with their children at every level! We don't need to be super-parents. Just people who see what God has given to us and take responsibility for its nurture and instruction.

For many parents, children are mostly a nuisance. These folks put out little effort trying to understand the moods, needs, feelings, or frustrations of their children. They may serve as a taxi service or a source of weekly income, but stop short of offering the deep involvement necessary to develop a child. Nevertheless, parents are leaders, and they need to take responsibility for the precious creatures given into their care. It all starts with seeking the Creator's help.

SEEKING GOD'S HELP

I've said it in many ways so far, but it bears repeating: the only way we parents can move from FEAR to TRUST is by seeking God's help. Good parenting can't be accomplished any other way—it can't be done apart from Him.

That's why prayer is so crucial to the parenting task.

Prayer is a powerful tool for us parents because it is always at the ready, in the hard times as well as the good times. So let's look closely at prayer and see how it can change our parenting. It can change the relationships between parents and children. And our own example of praying will also help our children learn what it means to seek God in their lives.

Teach Them to Pray

E.M. Bounds once wrote:

Be not afraid to pray; to pray is right;
  Pray if thou canst with hope, but ever pray,
Though hope be weak or sick with long delay;
  Pray in the darkness if there be no light;
And if for any wish thou daren't pray
  Then pray to God to cast that wish away.[2]

Prayer is direct access to God. Prayer assumes a belief in the very personality of God. It also lends itself to TRUSTing God instead of parenting out of FEAR. Prayer focuses our attention upon God's ability and willingness to hold fellowship with us. It also reinforces His personal control of all things and of all creatures and their actions.

One of the greatest lessons parents can provide for their children is the lesson of prayer. We began having "prayer times" early and often with our children and have always cherished the memories. And now our children have become praying adults.

Jesus' example and teaching inspire prayer. He prayed at crucial moments, showing His disciples the importance of communing with the Father regularly. Like Jesus with His disciples, we need to help our children understand prayer and enjoy its benefits. Here's what they need to know:

• *Prayer is conversing with God.* As early as parents can communicate with their children, they should be helping each child focus on God and speaking with Him. Psalm 4:3 says, "You can be sure of this: The LORD has set apart the godly for himself. The LORD will answer when I call to him" (NLT). David knew that God would hear him when he called and that God would answer him. Parents should help their children gain confidence in the fact that God listens, and that we can go to Him in prayer, for any reason, at any time of the day or night. Speaking with God helps children realize they have a heavenly Father who deeply cares for them and loves them—He hears and He answers.

Of course, any conversation involves both talking and listening. Let your children see you sitting quietly in God's presence, sometimes saying nothing at all. The Lord awaits our recognition of His constant presence. Usually it just requires that we slow down enough to listen.

• *Prayer reflects our dependence on God.* Genesis 25:21 reads, "Isaac pleaded with the LORD to give Rebekah a child because she was childless. So the LORD answered Isaac's prayer, and his wife became pregnant with twins" (NLT). Isaac and Rebekah had lived nineteen years together without having a child, for he was forty years old when he married Rebekah, and he was sixty years of age when Jacob and Esau were born (see Gen. 25:20; 25:26). Isaac entreated Jehovah, especially, for his wife. Some commentators think the words imply their praying together for this thing. God was pleased to exercise the faith of Isaac and have him become totally dependent on Him.

Teaching our children to pray helps them *realize the benefits of needing God. In prayer, children may learn how God works to meet their needs.* They can learn to sort through the differences between what they really want and really need. In this instant-gratification society, they also can learn patience and God's timing.

When teenaged Zachary began looking for a car, we committed the search to prayer. We had a family standard that our children could get a car under the following circumstances: (1) they had to qualify for a driver's license; and (2) they had to purchase it and pay for all insurance, routine maintenance, and gasoline. We paid for the big stuff, including tires, brake jobs, and other major maintenance items. This set of rules regarding cars taught them the value of saving, waiting, and praying.

We had prayed for months for Zachary to find just the right car. He had set up some of his own requirements for the vehicle, and we spent many a weekend searching. Finally we found one that met his needs, was under budget, and ran well. We praised God for leading us to the car that is still in use today and continues to be virtually free of major repair costs.

Zach had learned, by praying since he could talk, that God would provide in His timing. He was fully dependent upon God for the provision of a car, and God led him to just the right vehicle.

• ***Prayer is an opportunity to learn God's plan.*** The great Christian apologist C.S. Lewis seemed to know God intimately, but nothing taught him more than the loss of his wife, Joy. The movie *Shadowlands* is a moving tribute to the couple's loving but brief life together. However, a book he wrote after her death in 1961, *A Grief Observed*, is a better example of how Lewis dealt with the devastating loss.

In the book, Lewis moves from the "trough of despair" to a position where he recognizes that grief is a process, not a state. He learns that God has used Joy in his life and is now using her elsewhere (in heaven) for His purposes. It is a marvelous example of a man struggling with and believing in God's plan.

One scene from the movie sticks out to me. After the death of his wife, Lewis returns to teaching. One of his fellow professors asks Lewis about prayer. To paraphrase, the colleague asks, "Why didn't your prayers change God's mind?" Lewis responds, "Oh, prayer isn't intended to change God's mind; it is meant to change mine."

One Monday morning, Mary Kae reminded her mom about swim night and asked for ten cents so she could enter the pool. Money was tight for their family during those years, and there was not a dime for anything but the bare necessities. Knowing how much the activity meant to Mary Kae, her mother said, "Let's pray about this and ask God to provide a dime. If He wants you to go tonight, He will make a way."

The family prayed together after breakfast, and Mary

Kae went to school. She didn't think much about the evening events during classes. But on the way home, she was hoping with all of her heart that her mom would have a dime when she walked in the door. When she was about halfway home, her daydreams were suddenly interrupted. Several feet ahead of her on the sidewalk was something shiny, reflecting the sunlight like a mirror. A few steps later, Mary Kae discovered a dime, an answered prayer, and a lesson she tucked away in her heart for the rest of her days.[3]

What a blessing it is for parents to teach their children prayer—so they can begin to see for themselves how God works! Only through prayer can God change our minds and help us to understand how and where He wants to use us, or supply the "dimes" in our times of need. Prayer and Scripture reveal to us the wonderful works of a loving God.

Keep Them in Your Prayers

Lena is a marvelous book about a prayerful woman, a woman of unshakable faith, who constantly prayed for students. The author, Margaret Jensen, had a wayward son who chose in the late '60s to walk away from his family. She writes:

She [Lena] gathered me in her arms and I brushed my face against her black cheek and sobbed, "I might as well be dead." With that Lena straightened her shoulders and looked at me with those black eyes and said words that turned a light on inside me. "If God had wanted you to die for Ralph [Margaret's son], he would have asked you!"

"But Lena, I want my son saved!"

"Your joy got nothin' to do with what you wants. You joy am Jesus, child! You got Him, you got peace. You got Him, you got it all! Ralph not your business. His is God's business. Now I ask you, did the prodigal son's father call in the FBI or the police? No. He trusted God, and he waited. Now, Sister Jensen, you must unclog the channel. You get the long hair, bare feet, drugs, and that mess out that channel so you can see God. God's getting tired of hearing

*how bad the boy looks. He's lookin' at the heart. We begins
to praise the Lord till the joy comes.*"[4]

Lena prayed with Margaret, and eventually Ralph came to the
Lord and is now living proof of the power of prayer and the effec-
tiveness of "unclogging the channel."

We can relate to this in our home—literally. Our Jennifer has the
most beautiful red hair. It is thick and a wonderful auburn color that
shines in the sunlight. The problem was this: the effect, over time,
that washing her beautiful hair had on our plumbing. Every few
weeks I had to clean out the drain of her sink. Then, every few
months, I had to take apart the plumbing and unclog the channel
of red hair.

That is exactly what we need to do when we pray for our children. Just as Lena recommended to Margaret, we need to forget the
long hair, forget the earrings, forget the errors in judgment, and forget the behavior. We need to put that all aside and take the time to
pray, in earnest, for the hearts of our children. We need to do it
often, and we need to do it with passion.

Isaiah 7:12 reads, "Ahaz said, 'I will not ask; I will not put the
LORD to the test'"(NIV). God had asked Ahaz to come to Him, but
Ahaz refused. How many times do we put off praying for our children because we think God may not be interested in these little
details? Or maybe we're just too busy? Yet God cares and has told
us to come to Him. The channel is open. How do we do it?

• **Pray boldly.** When we approach God for our children (and
anyone else for that matter), we are called to come boldly to His
throne. "Such confidence as this is ours through Christ before God"
(2 Cor. 3:4, NIV). The word translated as "boldness" in this text
(Greek: *parresia*) was used of the free citizen of a city-state who
could say anything in the public assembly. It denotes the moral freedom to speak the truth publicly. Here, then, boldness describes the
confidence with which Christians can approach God because of the
redeeming work of Christ.

We can boldly approach God, asking Him for help, insight, and
the spiritual development of our children. This isn't a time for timidity but for frankness as we speak directly to the heavenly Father
with power, through Christ.

Hebrews 4:16 reinforces the idea, "Let us then approach the throne of grace with confidence, so that we may receive mercy and find grace to help us in our time of need" (NIV). When we look at our children and they feel they have failed, or when it appears to us that they are overwhelmed and need help desperately, we need never be afraid to approach the throne of God on their behalf. Jesus, fully human like us, will understand. Moreover, Jesus, fully God as is the Father, is able to aid us with all the resources of heaven at His disposal. It is important that we turn to Jesus as High Priest and realize all that He is able to do for our children.

• **Pray daily.** Psalm 55:17 reminds us, "Evening, morning and noon I cry out in distress, and he hears my voice" (NIV). What better way to get our priorities straight and take time to focus on the needs of our children? Daily bold prayer will cause change and help us to understand God's perspective about our children. It is a daily habit that will reap long-term rewards in the relationship. Matthew Henry writes, "In every trial let us call upon the Lord, and he will save us. He shall hear us, and not blame us for coming too often; the oftener the more welcome."[5]

• **Pray with authority.** "Now I Paul myself beseech you by the meekness and gentleness of Christ, who in presence am base among you, but being absent am bold toward you" (2 Cor. 10:1). Here Paul was into taking authority. Authority was given to him by the Lord "for building you up rather than pulling you down" (2 Cor. 10:8; see also 2 Cor. 12:10). Parents need the same authority—to build up their children rather than pull them down. They need to assume a position of family leadership and take authority, in prayer, for the safety and well being of their children. God's approach to authority operates on divine power. Through God's methods, Paul would be successful in "taking captive every thought" and making it "obedient to Christ."

We can take authority and ask God that every thought of our children be taken captive. Jennifer can testify firsthand to the power of this kind of authoritative prayer. During Jennifer's elementary and middle school years, Pam used to pray for her little girl—that when she struggled with temptation, she would be reminded of all the things we'd taught her. Pam decided early on to "take authority."

• **Pray specifically.** We parents need to approach God often, with a cleared channel, boldly and with faith, with specific requests. We shouldn't simply ask for blessings, or good grades, or successful relationships for our kids. We need to specifically ask God and then have the faith that He will deliver. "Let us go right into the presence of God, with true hearts fully trusting him" (Heb. 10:22, NLT).

One day in March, when we lived in Michigan, our children wanted to attend a Michael W. Smith concert. It was about ninety miles away, but it was a youth group event, and we felt they would be safe. As the evening progressed, it grew colder and colder. Then it started to rain, and the temperature hit freezing. The streets became sheets of ice, slippery and dangerous. Pam and I spent the entire evening in prayer for our children. We wanted them home, we wanted them safe. Believe me, we got very specific!

Well after 4 A.M. the telephone rang. It was our kids; they had landed at a youth sponsor's house, and the driver of the car could drive no further. Their stress level had hit the maximum. When we picked up our kids, they were tired but unharmed. Thankfully, no one in the youth group was hurt that night. We prayed specifically and we trusted. Did God answer?

"And I will do whatever you ask in my name, so that the Son may bring glory to the Father" (John 14:13, NIV). What a wonderful promise from Scripture! Jesus wants to know our concerns, and He wants to act upon them. We should approach Him with faith and specific requests. He will answer "yes," "no," "wait" . . . or change our minds.

The *Life Application Bible* notes for the Book of Colossians offers some wonderful specifics on how we should pray for others:

> • *Be thankful for their faith and changed lives (Col. 1:3)*
> • *Ask God to help them know what he wants them to do (Col. 1:9)*
> • *Ask God to give them deep spiritual understanding (Col. 1:9)*
> • *Ask God to help them live for him (Col. 1:10)*
> • *Ask God to give them more knowledge of himself (Col. 1:10)*
> • *Ask God to give them strength for endurance (Col. 1:11)*
> • *Ask God to fill them with joy, strength, and thankfulness (Col. 1:11)*

Prayer is a powerful tool for parents who TRUST enough to get involved. Prayer changes parents, and prayer changes children. It is the most useful tool for parental involvement.

Becoming Salt and Light

Parents, in order to get involved, need to make a difference in their children's lives. We can't just sit back on the sidelines and hope the kids "win" the game of life. On the contrary, we need to take responsibility, seek God's help through prayer, and assume a positive attitude that will help us make a difference. I call this becoming salt and light in our kids' lives.

What do I mean? I think of football player Joe Montana in this regard. Montana was a once-in-a-lifetime athlete. It seemed that every time he walked onto the field his team won. While guiding the San Francisco 49ers to Super Bowl victories he never failed to electrify the crowds.

Several things impress me about Joe Montana. First, he seems to be a confidently humble man. He does not swagger or brag. He just gets the job done. I never saw him be anything but a consummate professional. Secondly, Montana inspired his team. I remember seeing him return from serious, career-threatening surgery, and when he entered the huddle, the countenance of his team changed. Joe was back, and they now had the confidence to win. Basically, he made a difference to the 49ers. His quiet leadership helped the team rise from the brunt of jokes in the '70s to the team of the decade in the '80s. His style of leadership, preparation, spirit, and his ability to get the job done lent a significant tone to the team and to the game of football.

That, to me, is a salt-and-light story. But let's go into a little more detail, from a Christian perspective, about our salt-and-light responsibility for our children.

13 You are the salt of the earth. But what good is salt if it has lost its flavor? Can you make it useful again? It will be thrown out and trampled underfoot as worthless.
14 You are the light of the world—like a city on a mountain, glowing in the night for all to see.
15 Don't hide your light under a basket! Instead, put it on

a stand and let it shine for all.
—Matthew 5:13-15 (NLT)

In the time of Jesus, salt stood for three things:

• *Purity.* In the world of Christ, everyone thought salt meant purity. The ancient Egyptians believed salt was the purest element of all, as it came from the sea and the sun. Unfortunately in today's world, we are first-hand witnesses to a lowering of standards for purity. Everywhere we look, we see signs of once-high principles being dropped. From the dumbing down of textbooks to the low morals displayed on television and in movies, the bar of excellence has definitely been lowered. The parent who makes a difference by being salt and light must be the person who holds on high the standard of absolute purity in speech, in conduct, and even in thought. Christian parents can't withdraw their children from the world, but they must, as James said, seek to keep them "from being polluted by the world" (James 1:27, NIV).

• *Preserve.* Salt was used in Christ's time to preserve meats, and it was even used to preserve dead bodies. To preserve something literally means to keep it fresh. For parents to have maximum impact—to make a difference—they must display a fresh faith for their children to see and experience. John E. Crawford writes,

> *Being a real father [or mother] to your children is one job that no one else can ever do as well as you. Good fathers [and mothers] deserve their full share of top praise, for they are helping to build the loftiest cathedrals in the universe: young hearts and minds that are learning how to make this world a better place in which to live.*[7]

• *Flavor.* Let's face it, most food without salt is insipid and tasteless. Salt adds the zing, brings out the flavor, and rewards the taste buds. Parents who get truly involved and want to make a difference need to be to life (and their children) what salt is to food.

The Roman Emperor Julian once said, after asking to return to the old system of religion, "Have you looked at these Christians closely? Hollow-eyed, pale-cheeked, flat-breasted all; they brood their lives away, unspurred by ambition: the sun shines for them, but they don't see it; the earth offers them its fullness, but they desire it not; all their desire is to renounce and to suffer that they may come to die."[8]

What an awful statement, especially since Constantine had already made Christianity the religion of the empire! Parents who want to make a difference need to help their children continually discover the splendor of the Christian faith. In a worried world, the Christian should be the only person who remains calm. In a depressed world, the Christian should be the only person who remains full of the joy of life. There should be a sheer sparkle about the Christian, but too often we dress as though we're heading to a funeral, and we talk as though we just aren't allowed to enjoy the party. Whenever parents can, they need to help their children see the wonders of a life of faith.

We've spoken of salt, but Christian parents need to be light as well. Whenever Jesus refers to light, He usually is referring to Himself. Therefore, when He says: "Don't hide your light under a basket" He is asking us to be more like Him. What, specifically, did He mean?

• *To be seen.* Light, after all, is meant to be seen. I remember years ago driving across West Texas at night, as we drove to our new home in Michigan. We were "in the middle of nowhere," and it was pitch black. Our headlights provided our only vision, along with the headlights of the large semi-truck we stayed behind. Then, way off in the distance, we saw what appeared to be a small cluster of lights. The light was, in reality, over a hundred miles away, the place that eventually became our resting spot for the night: the city of Pecos. This experience reminds me of what parents should be for their children: a light that provides safety (as the truck did for us); a light they can always see (like the cluster of lights in the distance); and the light of rest (like the city with its motels).

• *To be a guide.* Light provides guidance. Earlier in this book, I mentioned how parents need to lovingly guide their children. It is a positive form of discipline to provide wise guidance. As a guide, parents can clear the way for their children. What obstacles are preventing your children from fully operating in their area of strength? How can you clear the way, provide the light, for them to see and appreciate their gifts and talents? What new life adventure awaits your children, and how will you guide them through it?

• *To be a warning.* Parents who TRUST enough to get involved will serve as a warning light for their children. A warning bell is too noisy and irritating; however, a warning light exposes the danger in a way that the child sees the danger and begins to build her own effective responses to it. It is always a tragedy when adults look back and wonder why their parents didn't stand up for them when they faced tough times. Parents don't need to nag or yell to make a point. Many times, they can just be that warning light, shedding illumination and information upon a troubling, confusing circumstance.

One of the greatest influences on my life was my fifth-grade teacher, Myrell Hendricks. Mr. Hendricks challenged us, motivated us, taught us, and served as an excellent role model. He understood who we were, and he took the time to get involved with us, understanding our passions, pushing us to do our very best every day.

When Pam and I became Christians as young adults, some dear friends invited us to attend their church. The first Sunday was wonderful, and it was announced that there'd be an all-church dinner that Friday night. Encouraged by the friendliness of the church, we were excited when Friday rolled around. We only knew one couple, so we were naturally a little nervous. When we walked in the door, whom did we see? Myrell Hendricks. My heart jumped in my chest, and I ran over to him and gave him a hug. At that moment, I realized why he was such a wonderful teacher. Not only did he take responsibility for us, he had no doubt been showering us with prayer all along. Salt and light did its fantastic work in my life.

How will it be for your own children? Author Alan Loy McGinnis observed, "There is no more noble occupation in the world than to assist another human being—to help someone succeed." Parents, get involved!

THINK AND TALK ABOUT IT

1. What results should parents expect when they pray for their children?
2. What are your five best traits or attributes? What are your children's?
3. What is it about darkness that frightens people?

4. If parents live as salt and light, how are their children likely to respond toward God?
5. Will you commit to pray every day for your children?

Notes

1 Tom Brokaw, *The Greatest Generation* (New York: Random House, 1998).

2 Edythe Draper, *Draper's Book of Quotations*, #8768.

3 Pam Vredeveldt, *Espresso for Your Spirit* (Sisters, OR: Multnomah Publishers, 1999), 81.

4 Margaret Jensen, *Lena* (Eugene, OR: Harvest House Publishers, 1985), 44-45.

5 *Matthew Henry Concise Commentary* (Database: 1996 NavPress Software).

6 *New Testament Life Application Notes and Bible Helps* (Wheaton, IL: Tyndale House Publishers, Inc.).

7 John E. Crawford, in *Men's Devotional Bible* (Grand Rapids, MI: Zondervan Publishing House, 1993), 1347.

8 William Barclay, *Daily Study Bible-New Testament* (Louisville, KY: Westminster John Knox Press, 1975).

Chapter 12

Trusting Enough to Let Go

AS I WALKED JENNIFER DOWN THE AISLE, I smiled bravely for the gathered family and friends. But inside, my heart ached with the dread of letting my precious daughter go. Jennifer and I are very close, and this day marked a happy and sad time in our special relationship, the day—it was August 9th, 1997—that would forever redefine our family. I know, it was a beautiful day for a wedding—but our little Jennifer was changing her name to Cook!

As I studied how I was going to learn to accept all of this, God helped me understand that letting go happens throughout parenting and that TRUST is essential at every step. Parents begin letting go from the moment of birth. They must learn to let the child sleep in a crib—alone. They must watch as the infant moves through the toddler stage to school age, and they fearfully look on as their little darling hops up into the school bus for the first time. School leads to sports or concerts or church outings, and soon it's time to let them drive. Talk about letting go.

Driving leads to dating and graduation. Then "the" event . . . and our family is never the same.

The important thing to remember is that letting go is a lifelong process. The events like marriage, graduation, moving out, and all the other major eventualities are just memorial stones. They are times captured in memory with pictures, relatives, and food (for the most part). TRUSTing enough to let go, however, is almost a full-time job for the parent. It starts early, and we might as well be prepared for it. So here we'll delve into three of the important aspects of letting go. First, there's a formula for letting go; second, there's the process itself, which we all need to understand; and third, there is a wonderful result to expect: an ongoing mentoring relationship.

THE FORMULA FOR LETTING GO

Understanding the formula for letting go will allow us to replace FEAR with TRUST. All of us are burdened by fear as we see our children pull away and stretch their own wings with their unique personalities, talents, gifts, and desires. We are FEARful of what will happen, not only to them, but also to us as our lives change along with their new freedoms.

Seeing our children drive solo was a real high point of FEAR for Pam and me. The mind can race far ahead of any rational thought as you see them pull away from the house for the first time. Future events do appear vividly real unless you can reach up to God and TRUST Him for the safety of your children. We need a formula to counteract our natural fears. I find a good one here in the Book of Luke:

> *1 After this the Lord appointed seventy-two others and sent them two by two ahead of him to every town and place where he was about to go.*
> *2 He told them, "The harvest is plentiful, but the workers are few. Ask the Lord of the harvest, therefore, to send out workers into his harvest field. . . .*
> *10 But when you enter a town and are not welcomed, go into its streets and say,*
> *11 'Even the dust of your town that sticks to our feet we wipe off against you. Yet be sure of this: The kingdom of God is near.'*
> *12 I tell you, it will be more bearable on that day for Sodom than for that town.*
> *13 "Woe to you, Korazin! Woe to you, Bethsaida! For if the miracles that were performed in you had been performed in Tyre and Sidon, they would have repented long ago, sitting in sackcloth and ashes.*
> *14 But it will be more bearable for Tyre and Sidon at the judgment than for you.*
> *15 And you, Capernaum, will you be lifted up to the skies?*

No, you will go down to the depths.
16 "He who listens to you listens to me; he who rejects you
rejects me; but he who rejects me rejects him who sent me."
17 The seventy-two returned with joy and said, "Lord, even
the demons submit to us in your name."
18 He replied, "I saw Satan fall like lightning from heaven.
19 I have given you authority to trample on snakes and
scorpions and to overcome all the power of the enemy;
nothing will harm you.
20 However, do not rejoice that the spirits submit to you,
but rejoice that your names are written in heaven."
21 At that time Jesus, full of joy through the Holy Spirit,
said, "I praise you, Father, Lord of heaven and earth,
because you have hidden these things from the wise and
learned, and revealed them to little children. Yes, Father,
for this was your good pleasure.
22 "All things have been committed to me by my Father. No
one knows who the Son is except the Father, and no one
knows who the Father is except the Son and those to whom
the Son chooses to reveal him."
23 Then he turned to his disciples and said privately,
"Blessed are the eyes that see what you see.
24 For I tell you that many prophets and kings wanted to
see what you see but did not see it, and to hear what you
hear but did not hear it."
—Luke 10:1-2, 10-24 (NIV)

Provide a Vision

The first aspect of letting go is vision. Verses 1-2 above show a picture of Jesus' vision for this group of ambassadors. He effectively painted a picture of the possibilities that were out there just waiting for them. "The harvest is plentiful," He told them; go out and do all you can do.

Providing vision is one of the most important things a parent can do to begin the process of letting go. Vision conveys hope with direction, encouragement, and believability. It is hope that the future is bright, regardless of where our children are today. Such vision helps them expand their scope. In addition, letting go is far easier when the parent has painted a positive vision and the child has responded. Nehemiah shows the power of vision:

> *17 Then I said to them, "You see the trouble we are in:*
> *Jerusalem lies in ruins, and its gates have been burned*
> *with fire. Come, let us rebuild the wall of Jerusalem, and*
> *we will no longer be in disgrace."*
> *18 I also told them about the gracious hand of my God*
> *upon me and what the king had said to me. They replied,*
> *"Let us start rebuilding." So they began this good work.*
> —Nehemiah 2:17-18 (NIV)

Parents frequently underestimate their children and fail to challenge them with their dreams (or to dream for themselves about God's work in the world). When God plants an idea in your mind to accomplish something for Him, share it with your children and trust the Holy Spirit to impress them with similar thoughts. Or, create in them the imagination to dream and cultivate their own vision for what God wants them to do. Often God uses one person to express the vision and others to turn it into reality. When you encourage and inspire your children, you put teamwork into action to accomplish God's goals.

Creating vision for your children helps them see the road ahead. It helps them see where they are going and reminds them that you fully support them in the things they're pursuing. As you together develop the vision, letting them go becomes a natural outgrowth of the process rather than a sudden jolt of dreaded reality.

When Jennifer was in college, she decided to move into an apartment. We planned her move together, and even though we were sad when moving day approached, we could face the change together because we had been part of the planning process.

Immerse Everything in Prayer

In Luke 10:2, Jesus tells His disciples to "ask the Lord of the harvest." He is encouraging His followers to pray about what He's sent them to do. We discussed in an earlier chapter the importance of praying *for* our children as well as praying *with* our children. Prayer is an essential part of letting go.

Mark 11:24 reads, "Listen to me! You can pray for anything, and if you believe, you will have it" (NLT). Here is a faith that realizes, that appropriates, that takes. Such faith is necessary if we are going to TRUST enough to let go. After painting the vision, we need to support our children in prayer, believing in God's attitude of love and goodwill toward them. Praying unceasingly is absolutely necessary as we watch them wander off into the new stages of their lives.

When we moved back to California in 1997, Zachary was to attend college in Michigan, our former home. We left Zachary the day after his nineteenth birthday, a month before he was going to start classes. We didn't have the opportunity to "see him off" or take him to his dormitory. We didn't have the privilege of sharing this new experience with him, but we did have the awesome power of prayer.

Our prayers were answered in two ways. First, God graciously provided Zachary with a Michigan "Mom." We are so very thankful that Thelma Sibley opened her home to Zachary and gave him a safe harbor for his college years. Thelma was there to help him when he started college, and we had complete peace that even if we couldn't be there, Thelma was there. Secondly, we prayed hard for a good academic start, and those prayers have been answered too. Zachary is now in the midst of a strong college career.

Always Be Training

In Luke 10:3-12 Jesus gives His disciples detailed instructions on what they are going to encounter after He lets them go into the world on His behalf. He knew they'd be facing hardships. He knew they left without food, money, or any extra clothing. However, he could confidently send them out because He also knew they were well trained. He had told them where to go and what to expect.

Training our children includes using every experience as a platform for learning. Each day can produce unbelievable opportunities to train children. A good biblical example comes through in the story of Joseph. God used so many instances in Joseph's life to "train" or prepare him for his future as second in command of Egypt. He was sold into slavery, became head of his household, languished in prison, and finally became prime minister. Along the way, God used every experience to mold and shape Joseph for his eventual leadership position and reconciliation with his family.

> *And so I solemnly urge you before God and before Christ Jesus—who will someday judge the living and the dead when he appears to set up his Kingdom: Preach the word of God. Be persistent, whether the time is favorable or not. Patiently correct, rebuke, and encourage your people with good teaching"*
> —2 Timothy 4:1-2 (NLT)

In the New Testament, as Paul reached the end of his life, he could look back and know he had been faithful to God's call. Now it was time to pass the torch to the next generation, to prepare others to take his place so the world would continue to hear the life-changing message of Jesus. Timothy was Paul's living legacy, a product of Paul's faithful teaching, discipleship, and example. What legacy will you leave behind? Are you training your children for the future when they will be let loose into the world?

Make Room for Testing

Jesus sent out His ambassadors and knew they'd be tested. The formula for letting go includes some testing so parents can see how their children will respond to various circumstances and people.

I can remember many times when we allowed our children to do something that stretched the former limits. These were planned, small "journeys" that gave us opportunities to train and guide our kids. Each time, when they returned or completed the new challenge, we spent time debriefing with them to see how they reacted, to find out what they did and how they did it. We wanted to know the results of the test so we could use it for further training.

Psalm 11:5 reminds us that "the Lord examines the righteous, but the wicked and those who love violence his soul hates" (NIV). God doesn't preserve believers from difficult circumstances, but He tests both the righteous and the wicked alike. For some, God's tests become a refining fire; for others, tests become an incinerator for destruction. In any case, do not ignore or defy the tests and challenges that come into your children's lives. We parents can help our children use those tests for their spiritual growth.

A test can bring out a child's true character. I think about Hezekiah in this regard. Second Chronicles 32:31 reads, "When envoys were sent by the rulers of Babylon to ask him about the miraculous sign that had occurred in the land, God left him to test him and to know everything that was in his heart." God tested Hezekiah to show him his shortcomings and to reveal the attitude of his heart. God didn't totally abandon Hezekiah, though, nor did He tempt him to sin or trick him. The test strengthened Hezekiah, developed his character, and prepared him for the tasks ahead.

It is good for parents, before they slip into the FEAR of letting go, to remember that God won't abandon their children, nor will he tempt or trick them. God calls parents to prepare their children for the time when He can use them to their fullest. He is with them wherever they go, in the midst of whatever they do. Parents who FEAR too much fall into a control trap; they risk hampering the full development of their children.

THE PROCESS OF LETTING GO

Once parents understand the formula for letting go, they must grapple with the process itself. The best way to begin is by observing how others have struggled. In the Bible, several couples learned to submit to TRUST as they let go of their children. Here are three of them:

Hannah and Samuel

Hannah was one of the wives of Elkanah and the mother of Samuel. Because she'd been unable to bear children for many years, she vowed to the Lord that if she should give birth to a son, she would dedicate him to God (sec 1 Sam. 1:11). Subsequently, she gave birth to the Samuel, and she fulfilled her vow by bringing him to the sanctuary at Shiloh, where he served the Lord under the direction of Eli. What was involved in the success of the process? Consider:

• *Prayer.* In 1 Samuel 1:9, Hannah takes her problems to God in prayer. She was being severely ridiculed by Elkanah's other wife, and in her moment of desperation, she prays desperately to God for help. She makes a vow to God, and verse 12 tells us "she kept on praying." Hannah was seeking God's help and specifically pleading with Him for relief.

She was "praying in her heart." She wanted this child, and she wanted it to be a gift to God. The process of letting go includes prayer from the heart and the willingness to allow God to have our children. We can't fully let go until we have the ability to speak to God and let Him know we are willing to let them go.

• **Dedication.** Hannah was dedicated to the Lord, and she dedicated Samuel to the Lord. " 'I asked the LORD to give me this child, and he has given me my request. Now I am giving him to the LORD, and he will belong to the LORD his whole life.' And they worshiped the LORD there" (1 Sam. 1:27-28, NLT). Samuel was probably three years old—the customary age for weaning—when his mother left him at the tabernacle. By saying "I give him to the LORD" Hannah meant that she was dedicating Samuel to God for lifetime service. For us, too, the process of letting go involves dedicating our children to God. Hannah was bold enough to pray; she was humbled by God's answer; now it was time to dedicate her son to God.

Many times the process of letting go is incomplete because parents forget this step. We have talked at length in this book about the special nature of children, that they are gifts from God and that they are "fearfully and wonderfully made." We need to take the next step and dedicate them, releasing them back to a loving heavenly Father.

• **Obedience.** Hannah had prayed and dedicated Samuel, and now she had to be obedient to the Lord. I am certain it took much strength for Hannah to fulfill her prayer vow. She knew in her heart what was right, but now she had to carry it out. That is still the task of parents today. We look at the circumstance, or we look at ourselves, and we forget the obedience part. We may also forget the benefits of obedience.

> *The Ten Commandments were given so that all could see the extent of their failure to obey God's laws. But the more we see our sinfulness, the more we see God's abounding grace forgiving us.*
> —Romans 5:20 (TLB)

It is only by God's unbelievable grace and Jesus' open arms that we could ever feel the freedom of obedience in our lives. It is only through prayer and reading God's Word that we can comprehend what He wants from us. Then we can experience the freedom to be obedient.

A drunk driver killed the son of some good friends of ours. It was a terrible time of anguish in their lives. The young man had been a model high school student, who served God in many ways. His parents, I know, couldn't have survived the awful tragedy if they hadn't been praying parents. They deeply felt the wounds of his death but also had dedicated him to God years before. So, in spite of their loss, they knew he was with God and serving God. Of course, they mourned their son's death and missed him greatly; however, they were also obedient to God's calling and began a wonderful ministry through Compassionate Friends and SADD (Students Against Drunk Driving). This couple is truly a model to all of us of prayer, dedication, and obedience to God.

Jochebed and Moses

Exodus 2 recounts the oft-told story of Moses and how his mother set him adrift on the Nile to save his life. Can any parent fully understand what Jochebed must have felt as she set the little basket into the Nile and watched her son float away? God is good, though. Moses' sister Miriam watched her brother and saw an opportunity to have her mother actually nurse Moses for Pharaoh's daughter, the woman who found Moses.

Jochebed let Moses go because she didn't want him killed by Pharaoh. She set him free, I believe, because deep down she knew from God that Moses would be the deliverer. Mothers are like that. And like Hannah, Jochebed seemed to understand the process for letting go. Two qualities surface as we study this remarkable woman.

A well placed faith. Jochebed placed her faith squarely on the broad shoulders of the loving God. She knew, deep down, if she trusted God, instead of fearing the Egyptians, that His plan would work for her. Her plan was simple; she put Moses in a strategic place so he would "float" into the area where the princess was. She used Miriam to follow the basket and make her bold suggestion of using the Hebrew woman to nurse the child. Jochebed trusted God for the rest.

A well-balanced faith. This mother didn't try to control things that were out of her control. Often parents try hard to take control of things that are beyond the reach of their powers. This causes unbelievable frustration and worry. How much better was Jochebed's plan! She trusted God for the things she couldn't control. She controlled the things that were under her control. This is a great partnership—God in charge of the uncontrollable and parents in charge of what they can control.

Years later, Joshua makes a great comment recorded in Joshua 24:15. He says, "But if serving the Lord seems undesirable to you, then choose for yourselves this day whom you will serve, whether the gods your forefathers served beyond the River, or the gods of the Amorites, in whose land you are living. But as for me and my household, we will serve the LORD" (NIV). He is asking the people to make a choice about how they are to be controlled. Do they want things other than God to control their lives? As we look at the process of letting go, we must ask ourselves the same question. We must decide if we want to be controlled by God in the process or want to worry and be fearful about things that are beyond our influence. The writer of Hebrews comes to the same conclusion when he writes,

> In the beginning, O Lord, you laid the foundations of the earth, and the heavens are the work of your hands. They will perish, but you remain; they will all wear out like a garment. You will roll them up like a robe; like a garment, they will be changed. But you remain the same, and your years will never end.
> —Hebrews 1:10-12 (NIV)

God never changes, nor should our desire as parents to let Him be in total control of our children's lives.

Mary and Joseph

> 41 Every year his parents went to Jerusalem for the Feast of the Passover.
> 42 When he was twelve years old, they went up to the Feast, according to the custom.

*43 After the Feast was over, while his parents were return-
ing home, the boy Jesus stayed behind in Jerusalem, but
they were unaware of it.*
*44 Thinking he was in their company, they traveled on for
a day. Then they began looking for him among their relatives and friends.*
*45 When they didn't find him, they went back to Jerusalem
to look for him.*
*46 After three days they found him in the temple courts, sit-
ting among the teachers, listening to them and asking
them questions.*
*47 Everyone who heard him was amazed at his under-
standing and his answers.*
*48 When his parents saw him, they were astonished. His
mother said to him, "Son, why have you treated us like
this? Your father and I have been anxiously searching for
you."*
*49 "Why were you searching for me?" he asked. "Didn't
you know I had to be in my Father's house?"*
*50 But they did not understand what he was saying to
them.*
*51 Then he went down to Nazareth with them and was
obedient to them. But his mother treasured all these things
in her heart.*
*52 And Jesus grew in wisdom and stature, and in favor
with God and men.*
—Luke 2:41-52 (NIV)

Luke gives us only one story from Jesus' youth. Joseph and Mary
were devout Jews who observed Passover in Jerusalem every year.
Three times a year the Jewish men were required to go to Jerusalem
to worship (see Deut. 16:16), but not all of them could afford the
trip. Therefore, if they chose one feast, it was usually Passover. They
tried to take their families with them, for it was the most important
event on the Jewish calendar.

When Jesus is separated from his parents, the lesson for us is
about letting go as our children go about their own business. Earlier
we talked about discovering our children's temperaments. We also

need to discover their gifts and talents. Finding what they love to do, and putting them in contact with these interests, is fundamental to letting go and TRUSTing God for direction in their lives. In this passage, Mary learns much about her son; in addition, she learns a vital lesson about the process of letting go.

Mary had to let go of her child and let him become a man, along with all that God had intended Him to be. Yet she searches for him out of fear, frantically looking after she and Joseph had left. It was not unusual for the men and women to be separated during travel; Joseph probably left later than Mary (as was the custom of the day) and thought Jesus was with her. She thought the opposite. However, they were looking for a boy, not the young man who was in the temple questioning the religious leaders.

It is hard to let go of people we have nurtured. It is both sweet and painful to see our children as adults, our students as teachers, our subordinates as managers, our inspirations as institutions. Nevertheless, when the time comes to step back and let go, we must do so in spite of the hurt. Then our children can exercise their wings, take flight, and soar to the heights God intended for them.

Release doesn't mean that parents simply cast out their children. It means giving children every chance for success. Our responsibility as parents is to provide support so our children can be released into what they want to do. This includes:

•An excellent atmosphere to live in. It should be positive, warm, open, creative and encouraging.

•Many excellent life-tools to work with. Children can't be effectively released if they are hampered with average life-tools (i.e., values, habits, and good priorities).

•A continual development plan. Growing children need growing and changing development plans; be creative!

•A vision to aspire toward. Provide your children with a positive vision of who they are and what they can do.[1]

THE MENTORING RELATIONSHIP

What can we expect as we let go of our children? In the Bible, men like David and Paul realized that the Kingdom couldn't be advanced by them alone; others were needed to help expand and build it.

They also realized when it was time for them to, in a sense, pass the torch. There's a time when we must pass the torch to our children, too, and TRUST enough to let go. But the process doesn't end there. In fact, it's the beginning of a wonderful new opportunity— the chance to keep on mentoring our children throughout adulthood. Let's look at Paul, in particular, as a prime example of this principle.

4 Brothers loved by God, we know that he has chosen you, 5 because our gospel came to you not simply with words, but also with power, with the Holy Spirit and with deep conviction. You know how we lived among you for your sake.
6 You became imitators of us and of the Lord; in spite of severe suffering, you welcomed the message with the joy given by the Holy Spirit.
—1 Thessalonians 1:4-6 (NIV)

If we are going to TRUST enough to let go, we as parents must do more than teach and encourage. We need to learn to mentor our children. In her book *Women to Women*, Sheila R. Staley points out that "the word 'mentor' originated in Greek legend, where Mentor was the wise and trusted counselor to whom Odysseus entrusted the education of his son. The mentor nurtures, supports, and provides wise counsel. She helps her protege set and realize goals. For the Christian woman, these goals are established and bathed in prayer. Growth emerges out of practical experience. The mentor serving as a wise advisor."[2]

Besides the call to mentoring, Paul speaks of conduct. The word "imitators" used here is the same Greek word from which we get our word "mimic." Paul was so sure of his own witness that he knew that if the Thessalonians just "mimicked" him, they would follow Christ as they built the church and lived their lives.

TRUSTing enough to let go, then, includes two more elements— mentoring and walking the talk. Some years ago, our pastor asked his congregation three questions: What do you cry about? What do you sing about? What do you dream about? Answering these three questions with your children is crucial for parents who want to mentor them and TRUST enough to let them go. From the knowledge gained, parents can help their children understand where they want to go and how they need to grow in order to get there. How better to help them move to a new level of maturity than by completely understanding the complexities of what makes them cry, sing, and dream?

Moving to a mentoring relationship also means we can help our children see their personal vision, set their priorities, and develop accountability. In a mentoring posture, we can work with our children to help them gain vision. We can help them lift their heads out of the day-to-day and up to a view of the horizon.

Eagles are wonderful birds, and God has bestowed them with unbelievable sight. Did you know that they have eight times more visual cells than a human being? This is what allows them to fly at such high altitudes and see small prey running in the grass or fish swimming in a stream. Mentoring can help our children develop exceptional vision. Letting go won't be such a difficult process if we take the time to help them develop "eagle-like" views of their futures.

Mentoring our children will also help them set excellent priorities. My mother helped me develop good study habits. By doing that, she mentored me into understanding the value of priorities. Priorities have to do with choosing what is right to do—and then doing it. A strong mentoring relationship guides our children into first understanding what is important and then knowing how to respond.

Finally, mentoring helps us develop a pattern of accountability in our children's lives. Letting go sometimes creates a vacuum in our children's lives. I do not claim to know much about physics, but I do know that a vacuum will never stay void. So, as our children move out and become more independent, what will fill the vacuum when their parents aren't available? Good mentoring will help our children feel the need to be accountable to other godly people and respect their wisdom and counsel.

The great missionary Amy Carmichael trained her children well. She loved them dearly, but she also held them loosely. Catherine Carmichael, her mother, also excelled at letting go. She had "an open hand" when it came to her children.

On a snowy January 13, 1892, young Amy heard God's voice saying repeatedly, "Go ye." After much prayer and soul-searching, she wrote her mother to tell of her call to the foreign mission field and to ask her permission to go. What would her mother, whose health was not strong, say to her? The great dangers of such a venture in that day and age—especially when undertaken by a young, single woman—were well known. Here is part of her letter in response:

> *Yes, dearest Amy, He has lent you to me all these years. He only knows what a strength, comfort and joy you have been to me. In sorrow He made you my staff and solace. In loneliness my more than child companion, and in my gladness my bright and merry-hearted sympathizer. So, darling, when He asks you now to go away from within my reach, can I say nay? No, no, Amy, He is yours—you are His—to take you where He pleases and to use you as He pleases. I can trust you to Him and I do. . . . All day He has helped me, and my heart unfailingly says, Go ye.[3]*

What a testimony of a parent who chose to let go! How many of us could have said "go ye" to Amy? No one ever said it was easy; however, if we take the time to TRUST and prepare our children, we can find God's plan for their lives and be able to say, with confidence, "go ye."

THINK AND TALK ABOUT IT

1. Which of your life goals or values would you like to see carried on by your children?
2. Share some stories that show, that from the small beginnings in the lives of your kids, you expect God to accomplish great things?
3. Why is it a good idea for parents to remind their children of what God has done for them in the past?
4. What are some of your prayer requests to help you to learn to let go of your children as they move into young adulthood?

Notes

1 These suggestions were adapted from John Maxwell, *Developing the Leader Within*

You (Nashville:Thomas Nelson Publishers, 1993), 131.

2 Taken from Novella Carter and Matthew Parker, eds., *Women to Women* (Institute of Black Family Development, 1996), 76.

3 Lindsey O'Connor, *Moms Who Changed the World* (Harvest House Publishers, 1999), 160-161.

Chapter 13

TRUSTING ENOUGH TO GET STARTED

DENIS WAITLEY WRITES ABOUT HIS MOM in his book *The Double Win*, recalling the quality and quantity of time she devoted to him as he grew up. "She listened to my big ideas and I loved to listen to her read to me from her collection of poems, some from laureates and some from her own pen." She wrote the following poem shortly after her three children left the nest and had gone their separate ways. Her words say much about the value of time.

Have you seen anywhere,
*   a dear boy and a girl,*
*   with a much younger brother of four?*
It was only today that barefoot and brown,
*   they played by my kitchen door.*
It was only today, or maybe a year . . .
*   it couldn't be twenty I know,*
They were calling to me to come out and play . . .
*   but I was too busy to go.*
Too busy with cooking and shopping to play,
*   and now they've grown up and wandered away.*
If by chance you should hear of a boy and a girl,
*   and their small winsome brother of four,*
Please tell them I pray, for to see them again,
*   I'd gladly stay hungry and poor.*
Somewhere, I'm sure, they must stop and look back
*   and wish they were children again,*
And, oh, to be wanted and with them once more,

I'd run out my kitchen door.
For there's never a task that could keep me away,
Could I just hear my children call me to play.
Where are my children?
I've got time . . . today![1]

Can you relate? So often time and circumstances take away our focus and cause us to look back with regret. I have talked to many parents who openly share with me the current problems they are having with their children. In many cases they will say, "My son is thirteen, and I cannot go back and start these principles you've been teaching. He won't even listen to me. I can't go back and start over." It breaks my heart to hear parents talk this way. I hear their frustration and their pain as they are trying to reach their children after much lost time. My advice to them is always the same. It comes from a friend of mine who once asked me, "How do you eat an elephant?" At the time I didn't understand what he meant, since I was deep in despair over a looming problem that seemed too big for any solution. As I sat there looking puzzled, he gave me the simple yet profound answer: "You eat an elephant one bite at a time." In other words, I couldn't solve my problem instantly. I had to begin solving it by taking the first small action.

This chapter is designed to help you get started in TRUSTing enough to parent. I hope you'll begin the process today, but always keep in mind that lasting change won't come about all at once. It could require many small steps; you could move forward a couple of steps, and then experience some slips. That's OK. The road to replacing FEAR with TRUST is full of turns, twists, and tumult. You will be under attack from the enemy the moment you begin, because he doesn't want you to be a TRUSTing parent. So get ready for the attack, and bathe your intentions in prayer every day. Celebrate the fact that you have made a decision to get on the road in the first place. And then determine to keep first things first with the best use of your time from now on.

PUTTING FIRST THINGS FIRST

Lack of time can block the moment-by-moment implementation of our plans for our children. It takes discipline to carry out what we desire to do, and there just seems to be less and less time in our lives to make it happen. E.M. Gray wrote an essay titled "The Common Denominator of Success." He spent his life searching for the absolute formula for success and found that it did not spring primarily from hard work, good fortune, or astute human relations. The one factor common to all who became successful was that they had the ability to put first things first. This required two things: the willingness to submit to a sense of direction and value, and the willingness to choose discipline over impulse. Following discipline over impulse is how we can manage our time for the children.

" 'The time has come,' [Jesus] said. 'The kingdom of God is near. Repent and believe the good news!'" (Mark 1:15, NIV). The time, prefixed by God, is now at hand. Jesus is proclaiming that the time is now, the time is fulfilled. The important point to remember is that God keeps time, and there is an appointed time for everything to happen. Knowing this, how should it change the way we spend our time?

"You saw me before I was born. Every day of my life was recorded in your book. Every moment was laid out before a single day had passed" (Ps. 139:16, NLT). Clearly the days are set aside for us. Our time has been ordered by a loving God. Years ago, I read that the average person wastes two hours per day. This is equal to thirty days a year, and before we are sixty-five, statistics tell us we will waste more than five years. Can we really put the right things first if we're wasting this much time?

I spend a lot of my time in retail, because that is my business, and I've noticed that people today don't shop like they used to shop. Mall visits are way down, the amount of time spent in the mall is way down, and the number of stores visited in the mall are down. The reason is time—people don't have time. No doubt Internet shopping is growing for many reasons, but one big reason is the fact that most Internet "stores" are open twenty-four hours a day, seven days a week. People don't have time, yet God tells us that our days have already been recorded. Are we making good time decisions within those days?

"Teach us to number our days aright, that we may gain a heart of wisdom" (Ps. 90:12, NIV). One answer would be to number our days. The word used here for "number" is a business word in the original language. It conjures the image of an old counting house, like Bob Cratchit's workplace in *A Christmas Carol*. It speaks to all of us that we should maintain the integrity of numbers. Time is a challenge, not because our days are numbered, but because we have the responsibility to make sure we are *properly using* our numbered, "counted" days.

In addition, the whole of Psalm 90 speaks of a person's transitory nature. David appeals to us to mind our time with diligence, as he himself asks to gain the "heart of wisdom." This phrase strikes a chord for putting first things first. Time shortages can block us into thinking we can't do something with or for our children, yet David seeks to gain the heart of wisdom. More than likely this involves significant prayer to ask God to help us weigh priorities and put things first that need to be first.

"See then that [you] walk circumspectly, not as fools but as wise, redeeming the time, because the days are evil" (Eph. 5:15-16). The average executive in the U.S. works sixty-three hours per week. Yet studies show that most people experience diminishing returns (in terms of concentration and productivity) after forty-five to fifty hours of work per week. Are we redeeming the time?

This phrase, "redeeming the time," literally means, "buying the opportunity." It is a metaphor taken from merchants and traders of the first century who diligently worked to improve sales and profits in the trading season. Managing time, therefore, is a talent given by God for a good end. It is misspent and lost when it isn't used according to His design.

How can we work to redeem our time? The enemy, circumstances, and lack of time can easily get in our way when we want to put first things first. We may have good intentions, but these roadblocks can pull our attention away from TRUSTing enough to get started down the right path with our children. So, how do parents break free of the barriers? How do we put first things first?

Choosing the Right Thing—and Doing It

There is a big difference between effective and efficient. The biblical Mary and Martha are good examples (see Luke 10:38-42). Mary stayed by the feet of Jesus—she was learning from the Master to be effective. Martha, on the other hand, was scurrying around the kitchen preparing the meal—she was being efficient, but not making effective use of her time (after all, Jesus was in her house).

The best way to put first things first is to choose the right thing to do. Jesus made this hard decision and then followed through by actually doing. Many of us have good intentions, but few people have learned how to master putting feet to their good intentions. Being effective is choosing the right thing to do. Being efficient is doing it.

Jesus Chooses to Preach

In the verses below, Jesus is just starting his public ministry. He had preached and now we see Him begin to heal and release people from demons. The crowds are starting to realize that this man has some great gifts. However, He chooses to do other things.

> *38 Jesus left the synagogue and went to the home of Simon. Now Simon's mother-in-law was suffering from a high fever, and they asked Jesus to help her.*
> *39 So he bent over her and rebuked the fever, and it left her. She got up at once and began to wait on them.*
> *40 When the sun was setting, the people brought to Jesus all who had various kinds of sickness, and laying his hands on each one, he healed them.*
> *41 Moreover, demons came out of many people, shouting, "You are the Son of God!" But he rebuked them and wouldn't allow them to speak, because they knew he was the Christ.*
> *42 At daybreak Jesus went out to a solitary place. The people were looking for him and when they came to where he was, they tried to keep him from leaving them.*
> *43 But he said, "I must preach the good news of the kingdom of God to the other towns also, because that is why I was sent."*
> *44 And he kept on preaching in the synagogues of Judea.*
> —Luke 4:38-44 (NIV)

In verse 42, He chooses to be alone, and in verse 43, Jesus tells the people that although what they want is OK, He had been sent

222 TRUSTING ENOUGH TO PARENT

for another mission. He had other priorities. Jesus had the ability to balance two priorities—He chose the right one, and then went away and did it.

The original language word for "must" in verse 43 means *it is necessary, there is need of, it behooves, is right and proper.* So Jesus chose what was right and proper for that moment, because it was necessary and there was another need greater than the one before Him. This was a huge choice for Jesus. It had many ramifications. It is important for us to understand this fully because many of our decisions on priorities have major ramifications on what we do and how we live. Choosing the right thing to do isn't easy, and it was not easy for Jesus either.

The decision for Jesus had major ramifications on how the Gospel message was to reach others. Jesus, at this moment of His ministry, could have chosen to fix Himself in one place and simply preach and heal. However, He chose to take the Gospel personally to many places. The new church was suddenly not tied to one area or one people; it was spread to the masses. Also, this decision puts emphasis on others' spreading the Word, not just Him.

I point all this out to show that choosing the right thing to do isn't easy and it will have potentially positive and negative conse-quences. This shouldn't deter us from making the hard choices, though. Jesus is a great model of making these choices. Pam and I made many difficult decisions as we reared our children. Taking Jennifer out of Christian school and putting her in a public school was hard, but I don't think any of us would look back and regret that decision. We chose to do what was the right thing for us—it was hard, we had some FEARful moments, but God honored our decision to TRUST Him.

Jesus Chooses to Pray

"Yet the news about him spread all the more, so that crowds of people came to hear him and to be healed of their sicknesses. But Jesus often withdrew to lonely places and prayed" (Luke 5:15-16, NIV). At this point Jesus makes another decision. Though His public ministry was so great, He chose pious retirement and prayer. For this moment, Jesus chooses the right thing to do and does it. He is efficient and effective.

Jesus had just finished a great healing miracle. In verses 12-14 we read about Jesus healing the man with leprosy. What a personal triumph that must have been! We are reminded that the news about Him is spreading—he is fast becoming a popular figure with unbelievable powers. It would have been easy for Him to begin a whole healing ministry. He could have set up shop and begun healing people right and left. However, Jesus chooses the right thing to do and does it. He isn't influenced by the circumstances now surrounding Him. Instead, He puts His public ministry on the shelf and gets alone with God.

When our children were small, the company for which I was working made me an incredible offer. They wanted me to become a Certified Public Accountant. I sat down and researched what I needed to do to achieve that certification. Since I was an economics major in college, I needed to take some additional graduate accounting classes, then I would need to take the CPA exam and spend two years in a low-paying internship for a CPA firm.

I went back to college, and though the first quarter went well academically, my time away caused some real strain on our family. The second quarter began and things just didn't seem right. Our children didn't appreciate all the time I was away from home, and my relationship with them was deteriorating. Pam confronted me one day to tell me how she felt. We took time to pray and to seek some counsel of friends. In the end, we chose to decline the company's offer. For that time in our lives, with two small children around the house, it was too much of a long-term risk. We had to choose the right thing to do (it was very hard) and do it (even harder). Looking back, we made the right choice. It was better for both of us, and our family, to do something different at that time. Jesus made a similar decision—it was right for him, at that moment, to be alone with the Father.

Jesus Chooses to Teach

"His mother and brothers came to Him, and they were unable to get to Him because of the crowd. And it was reported to Him, 'Your mother and Your brothers are standing outside, wishing to see You.' But He answered and said to them, 'My mother and My brothers are these who hear the word of God and do it'" (Luke 8:19-21, NASB).

In these verses, Jesus is presented with another set of priorities. He must decide whether to see His mother and brothers or stay with His disciples. Knowing that His time with the disciples was short, Jesus chooses to spend the time with them.

Jesus is demonstrating two things for us here. First, we see Him wrestle yet again with another tough decision. Choosing the right thing to do is never easy, and it isn't easy in this instance for Jesus. He must look at His mission once again and develop an answer that reflects His overall vision and goals. So often we parents see two competing circumstances and fail to choose the one that will forward our mission with our children. We put off today what we think we can do tomorrow. Jesus saw the disaster that would occur if He stopped working with His disciples.

Second, we see Jesus' loyalty to His disciples. What a vote of confidence and encouragement it must have been for them to realize that their leader was choosing to spend time with them—even when His family came to visit! We decided to stop the interruptions in our family times. We would regularly just let the telephone go to the answering machine when we were having devotions or reading to our children. This was such an important time, and the kids were so important to us. Our decision made them feel very important to know that Mom and Dad put their own lives on hold for a few minutes, just for them.

Martha Chooses to Ignore

As we look at choosing the right thing to do, let us look in detail at Mary and Martha.

> *38 As Jesus and the disciples continued on their way to Jerusalem, they came to a village where a woman named Martha welcomed them into her home.*
> *39 Her sister, Mary, sat at the Lord's feet, listening to what he taught.*
> *40 But Martha was worrying over the big dinner she was preparing. She came to Jesus and said, "Lord, doesn't it seem unfair to you that my sister just sits here while I do all the work? Tell her to come and help me."*
> *41 But the Lord said to her, "My dear Martha, you are so*

upset over all these details!
42 There is really only one thing worth being concerned
about. Mary has discovered it—and I won't take it away
from her."
—Luke 10:38-42 (NLT)

Mary sat near to Jesus. She was paying very close attention to Him. Martha, as we mentioned earlier, decides to focus on dinner. In fact, she chooses to "worry" over dinner.

The story of Mary and Martha can give us parents another important insight. While Mary chose to be the disciple, sitting at Jesus' feet, Martha chose to overwhelm Him with her dinner. Bible scholar William Barclay reminds us,

> *Think where Jesus was going when this happened. He was on his way to Jerusalem—to die. His whole being was taken up with the intensity of the inner battle to bend his will to the will of God. When Jesus came to that home in Bethany it was a great day; and Martha was eager to celebrate it by laying on the best the house could give. So she rushed and fussed and cooked; and that was precisely what Jesus didn't want. All he wanted was quiet.[2]*

Sometimes parents, like Martha, choose a course of action out of their own experience or need instead of taking their children's real needs into consideration. They are efficient in choosing but ineffective because they don't directly meet their children's need at the time. Our daughter Jennifer likes to tell a rather humorous (and sad?) story that makes this point. When she was in high school, one of her acquaintance's parents owned a car dealership. On her friend's sixteenth birthday, her parents gave her a brand new, white BMW. The girl, however, was most upset. "I told my parents I wanted a RED one!" she said.

Martha missed the mark by doing "something," but it was the wrong thing. Jesus was on His way to die on the cross. He knew He had little time to spend with His friends and disciples. Martha's kindness was well-intentioned but not well-placed. She chose the wrong thing to do, and she chose it out of her own definition of

Jesus' needs at the time. Barclay adds, "Jesus loved Martha and Martha loved him, but when Martha set out to be kind, it had to be her way of being kind which was really being unkind to him whose heart cried out for quiet. Jesus loved Mary and Mary loved him, and Mary understood."[3]

So, how does a parent choose? My point is that we are usually committed to doing the right things. We are committed to our children; yet, we choose wrong things and later regret our choices. Or, we don't even realize that we have made wrong choices. We fail to get inside our children's skin to see things from their point of view.

Getting Over the Barriers

Years ago I was introduced to the concept of the tyranny of the urgent. This refers to our tendency to manage time from crisis to crisis instead of planning, preparing, and choosing how to manage our time. Some time later, I would teach on time management and develop this chart for choosing the right thing to do and doing it:

	URGENT	NOT URGENT
IMPORTANT	BOX 1 Crisis Deadline-Driven Projects	BOX 2 Prevention Relationship Building Planning Recreation
NOT IMPORTANT	BOX 3 Interruptions Telephone Calls Popular Matters	BOX 4 Trivia Busy Work Pleasant Activities Time Wasters

BOX 1 is stress-driven. Too much of BOX 1 causes burnout, tension, cramming, and managing the family from one crisis to another.

BOX 3 is a short-term focus. It puts us out of control, and if we spend too much time in BOX 3, we can only develop shallow relationships.

BOXES 3 and **4** together lead to total irresponsibility. If we spend too much time in these two areas, we are making no intelligent choices for our family. We are choosing nothing that makes sense or meets needs. These boxes are also very dependent on others and serve to distract us from doing the right things.

BOX 2 is the heart of effective time management and personal development. BOX 2 stresses balance, discipline, and control. BOX 2 allows parents to build relationships with their children, not driven by crisis but by serving.

Therefore, it comes down to making decisions based upon our priorities in life. Do we want to spend our precious time with our children running from crisis to crisis, or do we want to choose, today, to do the right thing at the right time?

BOX 4 will bring us temporal pleasure, BOX 3 is always there to be a barrier to forging ahead. BOX 1 serves to strangle every last ounce of energy from us. BOX 2 is where we want to be and need to be if we are to choose the right things to do.

Remember: the seemingly urgent is rarely important and the important is rarely urgent. Now, it's great to be able to overcome the tyranny of the urgent; however, there are certain barriers that always seem to get in the way. Let's look at three of the largest. You see, once we get started, these three barriers serve to keep us from choosing the right thing to do and acting on our choices.

•*Barrier #1—Procrastination.* A dilemma sometimes faces parents. They are looking at a huge block of time involvement, or an overwhelming task, if they make a certain choice. How do you get started when something so large looms ahead?

To start an overwhelmingly large project, you need smaller "instant tasks" to get you started. Remember how we eat an elephant? Once we have made a sound choice, we may not want to do it all at once. Instead, we can choose the "Swiss cheese method." This method allows us to put small holes in the big slice of what is ahead of us. In effect, we nibble enough holes until, suddenly, the large decision or task isn't as big as it once appeared.[4]

As I have shared earlier, music has always been a big part of Zachary's life. When he was in middle school, he decided to play the clarinet in band. We started out with a rental instrument, then, when he entered high school, we bought an economically priced model. When he made a full commitment to band and the marching band, we purchased an expensive, excellent-quality clarinet for him. The Swiss cheese method worked for us. Instead of jumping into the big purchase before we knew whether he would even like being in the band, we just nibbled away at the demand for an instrument until we saw his complete commitment.

•Barrier #2—Being Under the Pile. All of us feel pressed and pressured under our unique pile of work and responsibilities. Every day, in fact, the pile just gets larger and larger, right? And that pile affects us as we attempt to choose the right things to do and do them. So, how do we get out from the pile?

Usually the pile is full of things that are, in reality, "C" priorities. They may be important, but not urgent, or urgent but not important (BOX 3 and 4 items). There are three kinds of C's. First there are "C" priorities that will rise to the top over time. They will become A's in a matter of time. Second, there are C's that are C's today, C's tomorrow, and C's the next day—they never rise above "C" level (maybe you need to live at the beach to appreciate that one). Lastly, C's will be Z's tomorrow.

The only effective way that I have found for dealing with the pile and de-cluttering myself from so many things that get in the way is to classify and prioritize the C's in life. It is vitally important to look at C's once and only react when they rise to a level of an "A" priority. This can free us from the pile and allow us to be free enough to choose the right things to do. Remember, only handle C's once.[5]

•Barriers #3—Interruptions and Crises. Every day has interruptions. This is a fact of life and can't be helped. Once we realize that, we can learn to control the controllable and accept the noncontrollable. We can't put a stop to interruptions, but we can set some limits:

• Keep them short. This is for non-emergencies, but when Johnny falls down, take the time to mend his wounds or take him to the doctor.

• Be ruthless with small talk. This especially is true with unplanned telephone interruptions.

• Learn to say "no." You can only be on so many committees before your family suffers. Your children come first.

• Always try to help the interrupter out in some way.

Crises are also inevitable. Here are some practical tips for handling a crisis:

• Use energy to explore solutions instead of losing your cool.

• Think about the problem—plan and run the crisis, don't let it run you.

• Take a "think break." Take time so you can mentally perform at maximum.

• Delegate what you can.

• Learn to take crises in stride. They are going to happen; you can't control the uncontrollable.

• Practice prevention. Even if they are inevitable, we can remove some things from our lives that typically lead to crises.

These barriers get in the way of effectively choosing the right thing to do and doing it. Parents who TRUST enough to get started will need to separate important from critical and then make effective and efficient decisions before moving forward.

Yes, it is possible to move ahead. Once parents understand putting things first and then choosing and acting, they are free to get started. Where you go from here will be determined largely by how much you allow God to use what He has created in you. The world is crying out for TRUSTing parents. Much will be required of you, but you are not on your own. God is your partner. The Lord is your shepherd. The Holy Spirit is your guide.

BECOMING THE PARENT GOD WANTS YOU TO BE

I've talked quite a bit about getting started, and I began the chapter by saying that you can only eat an elephant one bite at a time. In this last section, I'll suggest some small steps to help you get started. Yes, this is the Swiss cheese method. You may have a big obligation ahead of you. You may be one of those parents who has older children. You can't just jump in and assume things will change tomorrow. You will need to take some small steps. To redirect Neil Armstrong's famous comment, "One small step for parents, one giant leap for the Kingdom of God."

Here are some ways I would suggest that you can get started today:

Maintain a Positive Environment	You can, beginning today, create a positive and growing environment for your children. With it they will be able to learn and try new things. It will serve to create a very positive self-esteem.
Express High Belief in Them	Children can get discouraged easily. They will make mistakes and encounter things they don't understand. Expressing high belief encourages them to persevere, even when things get tough.
Pray for Them	Continual and frequent prayer can cause much to happen. Never underestimate God's ability to answer prayer. Hold on and let go. God is in control and prayer is a powerful weapon.
Recognize Their Strengths	It is critical that you seek to recognize their strengths and play to them. Children need a few wins under their belt and it accelerates the process when they can operate in the area of their strength.
Show Them How to Get from Here to There	Show them the way, systematically, to being people of God. It may be just simple things, but it is a lifelong road for all of us. Show them the road, tell them the vision.
Respect Them	Show them the utmost amount of respect. God made them perfectly, just as He wanted them made. They are special.
Find Them Doing Things Right	Try to stop finding all that they do wrong and praise everything they do right. Celebrate how far they have come, don't focus on how far they have to go.
Have Fun	In everything you do, find an element of fun. I hope that my children recognize me as someone who brought laughter into their lives.

Yielding to the Lord

To be the parent God wants you to be, you only need to yield yourself to Him. Let God show you where you can play a significant role in your children's lives as they stride onto the battleground that stands in front of them.

Satan, of course, wants you to focus on yourself and not on your children's needs. As a Christian, though, you have the Holy Spirit bidding for control of you and your children. Literally hundreds of choices you make every day will add up to the thrust of your life and theirs.

If you choose to use everything we have talked about in this book and everything God gives you to advance His Kingdom, He will only give you more so you can invest more. If you have a servant's attitude, God will trust you to manage more and more of His resources. Your children will be blessed and you will be blessed if you can daily seek His direction and care.

Most of all, God wants you. He wants you to be an influence within your family and especially to your children. He wants you to be an effective member of a local church and in the body of Christ. My personal advice to you is to be a parent of destiny. Help change the course of America's families by investing time in your own children. Do all you can to get involved with them, love them, understand them, and work with them. Begin to help them separate from your care (even if they are small) and learn to develop them for a lifetime with God. I ask that you pray for them, and teach them to pray. Most of all, I ask that you replace FEAR with TRUST.

THINK AND TALK ABOUT IT

1. What events or opportunities are coming up in which you can focus on helping your child?
2. What would be the first step for you in changing your relationships with your children? What will you commit to today?
3. What concrete action could you take this week to entrust the Lord with your future?
4. What FEARs will you cast upon God today?

Notes

1 Denis Waitley, *The Double Win* (Old Tappan, NJ: Fleming H. Revell Company, 1985), 186.

2 William Barclay, *Daily Study Bible-New Testament* (Louisville, KY: Westminster John Knox Press, 1975).

3 Ibid.

4 Adapted from Alan Lakein, *How to Get Control of Your Time and Your Life* (New York: Peter H. Wyden, Inc., 1973).

5 Ibid.